# INFORMATION SYSTEMS ANALYSIS AND DESIGN

# INFORMATION SYSTEMS ANALYSIS AND DESIGN

### Shouhong Wang
### Hai Wang

Universal-Publishers
Boca Raton

*Information Systems Analysis and Design*

Universal-Publishers
Boca Raton, Florida
USA • 2012

ISBN-10: 1-61233-075-4
ISBN-13: 978-1-61233-075-4

www.universal-publishers.com

Cover photo © Chris Lofty | Dreamstime.com

**Credit:** Visible Analyst is trademark of Visible Systems Corporation. Copyright of webERP is owned by weberp.org a trust of the webERP developers.

Library of Congress Cataloging-in-Publication Data

Wang, Shouhong.
  Information systems analysis and design / Shouhong Wang, Hai Wang.
      p. cm.
  Includes index.
  ISBN-13: 978-1-61233-075-4 (pbk. : alk. paper)
  ISBN-10: 1-61233-075-4 (pbk. : alk. paper)
 1.  Management information systems. 2.  Management information systems--Design and construction.
3.  Information resources management. I. Wang, Hai, 1973- II. Title.
  T58.6.W348 2012
  658.4'038011--dc23

                                                                    2011044241

# TABLE OF CONTENTS

*\*\* Electronic teaching material for this textbook includes model syllabus, sample exams, lecture PPT, and Visible Analyst project artifacts.*

# PREFACE

## Theme of Information Systems Analysis and Design

Information systems are vital to business. Information Systems Analysis and Design is one of the core courses in the MIS curriculum. It explains the right process of information systems development for the organization. The course also introduces the tools that can be applied to the information systems development. In the digital era, information technology has become a commodity, and the Information Systems Analysis and Design course has become a widely accepted elective course for all business majors.

The objective of this textbook is to help business students understand the concept of information systems development and develop practical skills of information systems analysis and design. Upon completion of the course, students should be able to analyze and design information systems in a professional manner.

Information systems analysis and design are connected with a wide range of topics. Generally, information systems analysis and design involves two interrelated parts: management of information systems development and techniques of information systems development. The techniques of information systems development include five major interrelated technical components: business process modeling, data modeling and database design, networking design, computer programming, and computer hardware and operating systems. Each of these technical components has its unique and plentiful material to learn. The fact is that a single course or a single textbook is unable to fully cover all these technical components. Commonly, management of information systems development and business process modeling are taught in the information systems analysis and design course, data modeling and database design are taught in the database course, networking design is taught in the data communication and networking course, and computer programming is taught in courses of computer languages. Hence, the primary theme of this textbook is management of information systems development and business process modeling. The secondary topics, including data modeling, networking, computer programming, and computer hardware and operating systems, are discussed very briefly in this textbook when delivering the monolithic concept of information systems development.

## Unique features of this textbook

There have been hundreds textbooks of systems analysis and design on the market. Given the long history of information systems, many information systems analysis and design textbooks were written decades ago and then revised for numerous times. The volumes of those systems analysis and design textbooks are usually huge since they contain many secondary contents that might be useful to know decades ago but are no longer essential for information systems development today. Many of those textbooks contain chapters that are rarely used for teaching and learning in this course. In the history of the management information systems discipline, systems analysis and design has been dominated by the computer software builders-centered approaches which were borrowed from the software engineering discipline. For instance, countless textbooks of systems analysis and design on the market still describe structured computer program design in great detail. In fact, structured program design was a major topic of systems analysis and design before the 1980s, but is no longer significant for systems analysis and design today. On the other hand, the fast growth of ERP systems and commercialized business software packages on the software market has shifted the strategies of information systems development from systems construction to systems acquisition in ordinary business organizations. Contemporary topics such as systems design for systems acquisition and acquisition decision making are lacking in the existing textbooks. This textbook emphasizes the concept of business-centered systems acquisition by including the contemporary topics, and aims to enhance students' practical skills of systems analysis and design.

This book maintains a good balance between the core concepts and the secondary concepts, as well as a good balance between the basic knowledge and the practical skills in systems analysis and design. The unique features of this textbook are summarized as follows.

(1) *Emphasizing information systems acquisition instead of systems construction*
The strategies of information systems development in the ordinary business organizations have been changed over the past several decades. Nowadays, except for software companies, few business organizations build their information systems

by doing programming and testing, because commercialized off-the-shelf software packages, services online, and ERP systems are widely available at low costs. This textbook emphasizes information systems acquisition, and provides a synopsis of information systems construction as supplementary knowledge. In presenting its contents, the textbook clearly distinguishes the two different systems development strategies.

*(2) Emphasizing the systems acquisition tools instead of the system construction tools*
Many tools for information systems analysis and design have been invented during the past several decades. The most commonly used tools in this field are: Data Flow Diagram (DFD), the Unified Modeling Language (UML), and Business Process Modeling Notation (BPMN). According to our experiences of teaching information systems analysis and design for longer than twenty five years as well as the research findings, we consider that the UML is a good set of software engineering tools for systems construction, but is difficult to use in the systems acquisition cases. Similarly, BPMN is a good tool for describing a business process at a detailed level for system construction, but provides little system perspective. DFD has been with us for a long time. DFD is not perfect, but is an excellent tool for students to develop system thinking skills for information systems analysis and design. As explained in the textbook, DFD is particularly powerful in the context of information systems acquisition which is much relevant to today's information technology environment of business.

*(3) Emphasizing contemporary contents instead of legacy contents*
Since the focal point of information systems analysis and design has been shifted from system construction to system acquisition in the contemporary information technology environment, this textbook eliminates legacy contents, such as structured programming design, which might be worth knowing for system construction but are no longer essential for business students. On the other hand, this textbook emphasizes contemporary contents such as selection of commercial software products.

*(4) Emphasizing project skills*

This textbook emphasizes the practical project skills. It provides a methodical guideline for information systems analysis and design projects, and describes the tools and techniques used for information systems analysis and design in a systematic way. This textbook is actually a comprehensive guideline for practical systems analysis and design projects. As specified in Appendix A, the general requirement for students, who learn information systems analysis and design using this textbook, is a real-world information system analysis and design project.

*(5) Eliminating secondary material*

This textbook eliminates secondary material that is not essential to business students for learning information systems analysis and design. It has little overlap with other independent information systems textbooks such as database design and implementation, data communication and networking, and computer programming languages. All chapters and appendices of this textbook are necessary for the systems analysis and design course.

**The organization of this textbook**

The textbook has seven chapters, plus appendices. Chapter 1 introduces students into the information systems analysis and design field, and discusses the roles of systems analysts in business organizations. Chapter 2 discusses information systems development strategies, and presents a general overview of the project management for information systems development. Chapter 3 explains the systems planning phase. Chapter 4 provides details of the systems analysis process and DFD, a powerful tool for systems analysis. Chapter 5 presents details of the systems design process. Chapter 6 explains the systems implementation and conversion process. Chapter 7 is an overview of post-project activities and information systems maintenance. Each chapter includes a list of key terms that convey the important concepts of information systems analysis and design. Exercise instructions for course projects are also listed at the end of each relevant chapter. The book includes four appendices that are relevant to the course project of systems analysis and design. Appendix A provides a thorough guideline for the course project of information systems analysis and design. Appendix B is a short tutorial of CASE tool Visible Analysis. Appendix C is an example of systems analysis and design case. This example is not a complete project report, but provides the key features of a typical information systems analysis and design project for small business. Appendix D exhibits an example of open source ERP system. The samples of user interfaces are useful for students to learn how to examine application software products for system acquisition. Finally, this textbook includes a set of PPT slides handouts for students to review the textbook material conveniently.

In summary, this textbook is designed for business undergraduate students in all majors who study information systems analysis and design for business organizations.

Shouhong Wang, PhD
University of Massachusetts Dartmouth

Hai, Wang, PhD
Saint Mary's University

# CHAPTER 1. INTRODUCTION

## 1.1. Context of Information Systems Analysis and Design

An **information system** is an organized collection of people, information technology, information resources, and all coordinated activities to achieve certain objectives in the business organization. Conceptually, an information system may or may not be computerized. For instance, in a manual inventory process system, the set of the inventory bookkeepers, calculators, and pencil and paper are the information system. Practically, nowadays computers have become an indispensable element of contemporary information systems. As information technology is essential and vital to business, the development of an information system in the organization becomes crucial for the success of the organization. This textbook disseminates theories and methodologies of the process of information systems development.

**Information systems analysis and design** refers to the process of completing an information system development project. **Information systems development** covers a wide range of technical areas including business process modeling, data modeling and database design, networking design, computer programming, and computer hardware and operating systems. Each of these areas discusses its subjects of information systems in addition to information systems development, and has rich and unique material to learn. For instance, the theories of data modeling and database design can be applied to data resource management and business intelligence in addition to information systems development. The fact is that it is impossible for a single course or a single textbook to fully cover all these areas. Practically, the information systems analysis and design course and its textbook focus on two components: management of information systems development and business process modeling, and touch on other technical areas very briefly when delivering the monolithic concept of information systems development. The context of the information systems analysis and design course is depicted in Figure 1.1.

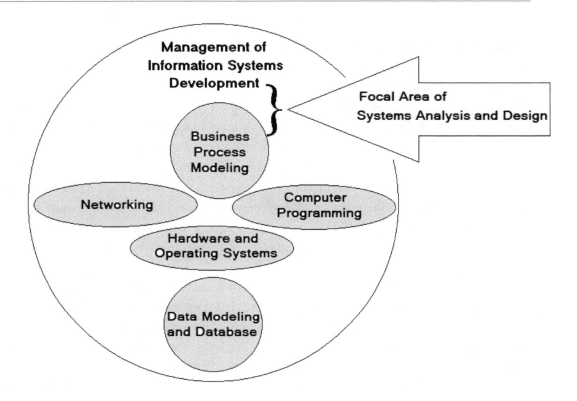

**Figure 1.1. Context of Information Systems Analysis and Design**

## 1.2. Central Objective of Information Systems

The central objective of an information system is to create **value** for the organization by using information technology. For most business firms, value means more profits. For non-for-profit organizations and government agencies, value can mean much more than monetary measures.

In the information systems literature and on the Web, you can find countless success stories of information systems development, and you can also read many failure cases of information systems development. There are many factors that can have impact on the outcomes of information systems development. The commonly considered **success factors** for the information systems development are:

- Top management support;
- User involvement;
- Alignment of the business strategy and the project strategy;
- Effective project management;
- Organizational collaboration; etc.

Clearly, in terms of success factors, an information systems development project is not much different from any types of projects such as highway projects and green energy projects. However, an information systems development project is significantly different from other types of projects in that the value created by the information system is difficult to measure before the information system actually takes place. On the other hand, to justify an information system development project, the organization must estimate the potential value produced by the information system. The process of information systems analysis and design is to provide an accurate estimation of the potential value of the information system and to ensure the potential value of the new information system.

## 1.3. Systems Analysts

A **systems analyst** is a person who is responsible for the development of an information system. A systems analyst must understand the three aspects of information systems development: the business, information technology, and the people. She/he must possess business skills, information technology skills, and human interaction skills to fill her/his job responsibilities.

### 1.3.1. Business skills

The systems analyst must have a clear vision of the business environment and the business strategy of the organization. She/he must understand the nature of the business and the business processes in the organization. When working on the system development, the systems analyst must consider the various factors of the business environment and an alignment of the information system with the business strategy.

### 1.3.2. Information technology skills

The systems analyst must have solid knowledge of contemporary information technology, as well as fluent practical skills of systems analysis and design. The team of systems analysts of the organization possesses the best knowledge about how the organization can apply information technology to support the day-to-day operations and decision making at all managerial levels to achieve the organization's goal.

### 1.3.3. Human interaction skills

The systems analyst must understand the users' needs for the information system and be able to involve the users in the information system development process. Dealing the relationships with users, training users, and conducting surveys and interviews are an important part of the job of the systems analysts.

### 1.3.4. Managerial skills

The systems analyst needs to manage people, pressure, and risks. She/he must demonstrate the leadership in the project team as well as the analytical capability of problem solving. The systems analyst must deal with co-workers, managers, and systems users fairly, honestly, and ethically.

Apparently, the skills set of systems analysts is an integration of soft-skills (e.g., human interactions) and hard-skills (e.g., systems analysis and design). The job titles of systems analyst vary depending on the focal skills needed for the special programs. Business analyst, program analyst, change management analyst, and information technology specialist are the alternative job titles of systems analyst. A business analyst focuses on the business issues surrounding the information system. Program analyst is a broad job title. If a position of program analyst is set for information systems development, the program analyst focuses on the business process and the coordination among functional areas in the course of information systems development. A change management analyst focuses on the issues of changes caused by the new information system, including the new policies, new procedures, user training, and system support in the organization. Information technology specialist is another broad job title for specialists of modern digital technology. Upper management positions in the career path of systems analyst include information systems project manager, information systems manager, and chief information officer (CIO).

### *Key Terms*

Information system

Information systems analysis and
   design

Information systems development

Value

Success factors for information
   systems development

Systems analyst

Skill set of system analyst

# CHAPTER 2. INFORMATION SYSTEMS DEVELOPMENT

This chapter provides an overview of the systems development life cycle model and an overview of information systems development project management. It discusses three fundamental information systems development strategies: systems acquisition, systems construction, and outsourcing.

## 2.1. Systems Development Life Cycle

The **systems development life cycle** (**SDLC**) is a conceptual model of the phases an information system goes through. The typical systems development life cycle model suggests five fundamental phases of information systems development process: planning, analysis, design, implementation, and maintenance, as depicted in Figure 2.1.

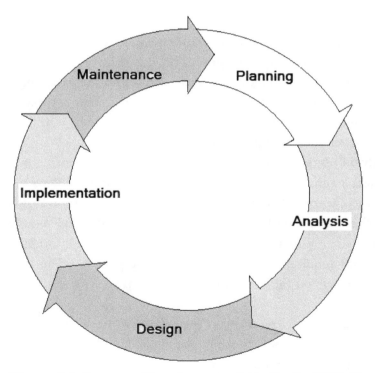

**Figure 2.1. Systems Development Life Cycle (SDLC)**

The SDLC model provides a general guideline for the information systems development in two aspects.

(1) The system development process of an information system must move through these five phases. Although the pattern of how an information system goes through these phases depends on the approach used for the information system development, as discussed in detail in the following chapters of this book, a successful information systems development process can never omit any of these five phases.

(2) Each of these five phases produces a set of products, called **deliverable**, which is used as the input to its successor phase. Each phase elaborates on the work of its predecessor phase. The structures and forms of the deliverables of each phase can vary depending on the approaches used for the information system development. The quality of the deliverables affects the quality of the entire information system development project.

The **planning phase** is the process of preliminary investigation to understand *why* a new information system should be created for the organization. The deliverable of the planning phase includes a report of the feasibility study and the workplan for the new information system development project. Once the organization decides to create a new information system, a full-scale project of information system development is then started.

The **analysis phase** is the first stage of the full-scale information system development project to investigate *what* the new information system will do. In this phase, the project team fully investigates the current information system (or the **as-is** system) of the organization and the specific business needs (or the **system requirements**) for the new information system. The new information system that meets the system requirements is called the **to-be** system. The deliverable of the analysis phase reports on the following major system analysis results.

- The differences between the as-is system and to-be system;
- The system requirements for the to-be system;
- The strategy of system development for the design phase.

The deliverable of the system analysis phase actually presents a blueprint for the new information system.

The **design phase** determines *how* the to-be system will be created and *how* it will operate in terms of hardware, software, networking, system personnel, and operational procedures. The deliverables of the design phase are the detailed **system specifications** of system infrastructure, hardware, software, and networking for the implementation phase. The design phase actually provides the solution to the to-be system.

The **implementation phase** builds the new information system based on the system specifications provided by the design phase. The methods applied to the system implementation phase vary depending on the strategies of systems development, as discussed in detail later in this book. By the end of the implementation phase, the new information system replaces the old information system.

The business environment changes constantly. Also, the newly built information system might need improvement. The **maintenance phase** improves the new information system. Because of the innovation of information technology and significant changes of the business environment, the cost of system maintenance eventually becomes unjustified at a certain point. The next generation of information system in the organization will be inevitable. The information system development starts a new cycle.

## 2.2. Management of Systems Development Project

The management of information systems development projects has unique characteristics in some aspects in comparison with the management of other types of projects, as discussed below.

### 2.2.1. Project sponsor and project approval

An information system project in the organization must have its **project sponsor** who holds a top position in the organization (e.g., VP). The project sponsor has an interest in the project and is involved in the entire project duration. An information system project must be approved by the organization which will commit the resources and support to the project. The project approval procedure must comply with the structure and the rules of the organization.

### 2.2.2. Project scope definition, project scale estimation, and risk assessment

An information system is an open system which means that it is interconnected to other systems, as the business processes in the organization are interconnected each other and are linked to the systems of other organizations. It is necessary to define the scope of the information development project before it starts. The **project scope** defines the range of system requirements of the organization for the new information system. For example, a new retail information system project covers the system requirements of sales and purchasing information processes, but does not cover the system requirements of shipping information processes because its shipping jobs are outsourced to another shipping company. In this example, the project scope includes the functions of sales and purchasing, but excludes the functions of shipping.

A phenomenon called **scope creep** happens when new components are added to the project after the scope has been defined. It is common in the information technology industry because some additional components are hard to ignore for many reasons. Nevertheless, the project administrator must control scope creep to, say, less than 5% of the original project scope.

Once the project scope has been determined, the **project scale**, in terms of the budget, the time duration, and the manpower that will be involved in the project, must be estimated. For the time being, there is no accurate method for project scale estimation. A common practice is to survey the industry to find similar information system projects and to collect data for estimation.

Any project can have a **risk** of failure that the new information system fails to delivery on time as planned and significant negative consequences occur. Risk assessment is to document each of the potential risks by explaining the nature of the risk, the likelihood of the risk, the potential damage caused by the failure, and possible solutions.

### 2.2.3. Project team management

The project team is crucial for the success of the project. Highly qualified and self-motivated team-players with fluent systems analysis and design skills are the prerequisite for the achievable project goals. In the information technology field, the turn-over rates of information systems professionals are high. This fact raises two major challenges for the information systems project management.

(1) The project manager must apply pertinent rewarding methods to motivate the information systems professionals, such as recognition, advancement, and self-regulation.

(2) The project team must promote knowledge sharing and collaboration among the team members through the use of **CASE** (**Computer Aided Systems Engineering**) tools and Web2.0 techniques (e.g., blogs, wiki, etc.).

### 2.2.4. Project control and coordination

There are many generic project management software packages on the market (e.g., Microsoft Project) that can be used for the information systems project control and coordination. Many general activities of project control and coordination, such as compiling the workplan of project and generating a Gantt chart or a PERT chart for the time management, can be supported by these generic project management software packages. However, the generic project management software packages have little support for the unique activities of information system projects such as ensuring the **system standards** (e.g., using the consistent formats and terminologies for documentation). Thus, CASE tools must be used in addition to the generic project management software packages for the effective information systems project management. Appendix B in this book discusses CASE tools in detail.

### 2.3. Fundamental Strategies of Information Systems Development

Information systems analysis and design lies in the core of the information systems discipline. The general strategies, approaches, and techniques of systems analysis and design are continually renovated. Decades ago, information system projects were more likely to place the focal point on the use of databases and computer programming languages to construct computerized information systems. Gradually, **off-the-shelf software packages** and **ERP (Enterprise Resource Planning)** systems are widely available on the market for business organizations to develop information systems without construction from scratch. Business organizations and information technology consultants have found that the use of commercialized software products has huge advantages over the in-house construction of information systems. Recently, many service companies provide the information process services through the Internet, called **Software as a Service** (**SaaS**), which allow business organizations to use the provided services without having their own information systems. In the near future SaaS will become more popular because of the **cloud computing** technology which provides computation, software, data access, and storage services on the Internet without requirement for the end-user knowledge of the physical location and configuration of the system of the services providers.

Nowadays almost all types of business applications, with few exceptions, can be implemented by using ERP systems or off-the-shelf software packages (see Figure 2.1). Except for companies on the cutting-edge of information technology innovations, virtually no ordinary business organization would construct an information system using basic tools such as computer programming languages. In fact, the system construction for a practical business application with a reasonable scope is time consuming, risky, costly, and technology demanding.

An **information systems development strategy** is a plan of action designed to allow the organization to concentrate its limited resources on the greatest opportunities of information system development. There are three fundamental information systems development strategies for ordinary business organizations: systems acquisition, systems construction, and outsourcing, as discussed below.

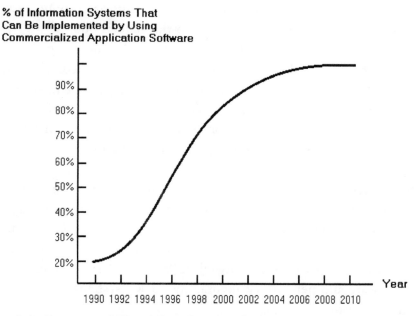

**% of Information Systems That
Can Be Implemented by Using
Commercialized Application Software**

**Figure 2.1. Commercialized Application Software Market Has Matured**

### 2.3.1. Systems acquisition

As a result of the proliferation of commercialized business applications software, systems construction is no longer the major focal point of information systems analysis and design. Instead, seeking the strategic value of information systems for the business has become the central task of information systems analysis and design.

Nowadays the first strategy of information systems development for an ordinary business organization to consider is **systems acquisition**, which means that the organization uses commercialized business applications software products for its new information system. Generally, there are three types of business applications software products for the systems acquisition development: off-the-shelf software packages, ERP systems, and SaaS, although the cut-line between off-the-shelf software packages and ERP systems can never be sharp.

(1) An **off-the-shelf software package** refers to a software product that is ready-made and available for sale, lease, or license to the general public. An off-the-shelf software package is designed for a particular type of business (e.g., restaurant, car repair, retail shop, etc.), and is simple to use for small or medium-sized business organizations. The producer of an off-the-shelf software package or the vendors can provide maintenance and user training services. Usually, an off-the-shelf software package has a limited capability of customization for very special needs. If an off-the-shelf software package is **open source**, it is free to use but has no liability.

(2) An **ERP system** integrates internal and external management information across an entire organization, embracing finance/accounting, manufacturing, sales and service, inventory management, CRM, etc. Its purpose is to facilitate the business processes of all business functions inside the boundaries of the organization and manage the connections to outside organizations. An ERP system can run on a variety of hardware and network configurations. ERP systems typically include the following characteristics.
- An ERP system is an integrated system that operates in real time.
- An ERP system has a common database which supports all applications.
- An ERP system is a set of modules with consistent appearance.
- An ERP system can be used for all types of large business organizations; however, significant work of configuration or even customization is needed to fit specific requirements for individual organizations. For instance, the configuration facility of an ERP system would allow the client organization to choose currency system, metric system, LIFO or FIFO for cost accounting, and so on.

Usually, the information system development team should include specialists trained by the ERP system provider for the ERP system configuration and customization.

Recently, there are many open source ERP systems (see an example in Appendix D). A business model behind open source ERP systems is the win-win relationship between the business community, the partner network, and the software editors. The partners are intended to create the market around the open source ERP system and to create services. The software editors are responsible for the quality and the vision on the development of the ERP system. The business community generates activities and contributes to the growth of the ERP system. All modules produced by the software editors, the partners and the community are to be open source. The user of an open source ERP system does not automatically receive system support and services directly from anyone. However, an open source ERP system has its active social network that can create service offers and deals.

(3) **SaaS** is a software delivery model in which application software and its associated data are hosted centrally by the service provider and are typically accessed by the customers using Web browsers over the Internet. SaaS applications have the following characteristics.

• A SaaS application can support configuration, but not customization.

• A SaaS application can be upgraded quickly.

• Many SaaS applications offer features that allow its customers to collaborate and share information.

• A SaaS application is hosted in cloud, and response time and data security could be issues for customers.

The systems acquisition strategy makes it possible for the organization to develop its new information system in a short period at a low cost. Because of the advantages of the systems acquisition strategy, the methodology of systems analysis, design, and implementation has been shifted away from the traditional builder-centered approaches. Nowadays the central task of system development is the selection of a commercialized software product that has the best match of its functions and features to the system requirements.

Generally, the information systems acquisition development approach follows the classical SDLC model closely. However, the concept of each phase of the SDLC model in the systems acquisition development approach is quite different from that in the systems construction development approaches. The general course of systems acquisition development is illustrated in Figure 2.2.

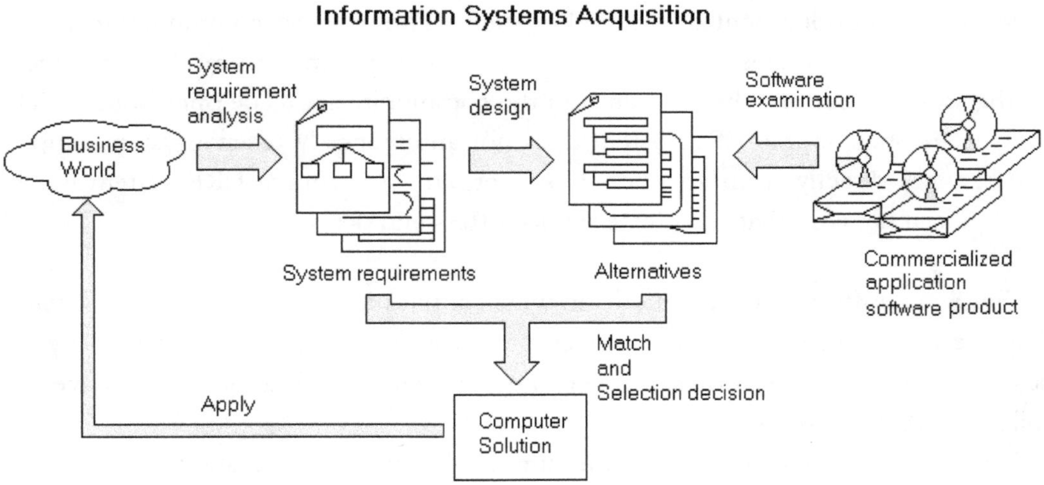

**Information Systems Acquisition**

**Figure 2.2. Information Systems Acquisition Development**

## 2.3.2. Systems construction

A new information system of the organization can be constructed in-house by using computer programming tools and database management systems. The **systems construction** strategy was common decades ago, but today it is applicable only to organizations with very unique requirements. Software providers and information technology pioneers (e.g., Google) must adopt this systems development strategy because no commercialized software products are available on the market that can meet their requirements. Using the systems construction strategy, the systems analysis and design team must generate construction specifications for the system implementation, as illustrated in Figure 2.3.

Apparently, constructing an information system takes a considerable time and resources. Since the newly built information system has not been used before, rigorous and intensive tests must be performed before it can be used, or errors are inevitable.

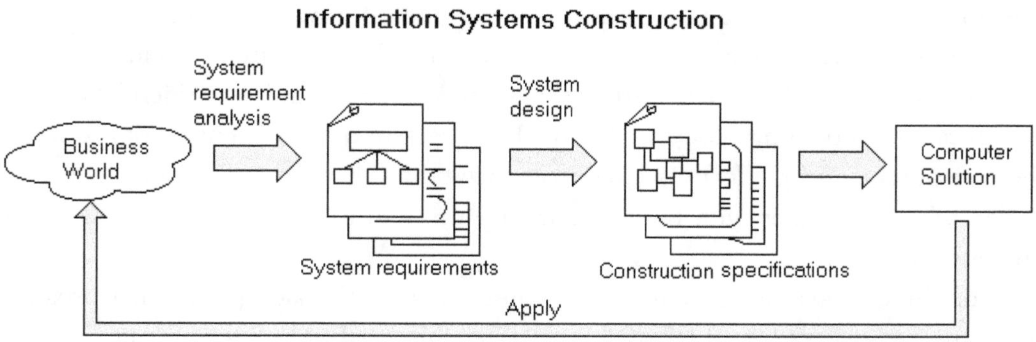

## Information Systems Construction

**Figure 2.3. Information Systems Construction Development**

Given the fact that few business students will choose the careers in information systems construction, this textbook emphasizes the core subject of systems acquisition for the information systems analysis and design course for all business majors, while discusses systems construction concisely.

### 2.3.3. Outsourcing

The third information systems development strategy is **outsourcing**. Outsourcing, in the context of systems analysis and design, is the contracting out of the systems development jobs to an external service provider(s). Organizations that outsource their systems development jobs seek cost savings in system development, focus on their core business, and access to contemporary intellectual property and wider experience and knowledge.

To initiate an information systems development project through outsourcing, a large organization, especially a government agency, uses a form of **Request for Proposal (RFP)** to search the best service provider for the systems development project. For smaller projects with smaller budgets, a **Request for Information (RFI)**, a shorter and less detailed request, can be used. When the request is so complete that the vendor needs only provide a price, a **Request for Quote (RFQ)** could be sufficient.  Often, small and medium-sized organizations simply hire trustable vendors or consultant firms to develop the information systems for them.

The downside of outsourcing for the outsourced organizations includes loss of managerial control, hidden costs, threat to security and confidentiality, and complicated contracting process.  Although the system development work is done by the outsourcing firm, the outsourced organization still needs to appoint a project liaison who cooperates with the outsourcing firm and monitors the progress of the outsourced project.

The three fundamental systems development strategies along with their pros and cons are summarized in Table 2.1.  Clearly, this textbook teaches how one can develop information systems for her/his company or her/his client, and the main standpoint of this textbook is "insourcing".  In the rest part of this textbook, outsourcing is pulled out from the discussion.

## 2.4. Diversified Information System Construction Approaches

The concepts of major system construction approaches are worth understanding, although few ordinary business organizations apply the systems construction strategy today.  There have been diversified **system construction approaches** to information system construction in the perspective of the SDLC model.

### 2.4.1. Waterfall approach

The traditional approach to constructing a new system follows the classical SDLC model, and is called the **waterfall approach**, as shown in Figure 2.4.  The major advantage of the waterfall approach is that each phase of the development process produces a clear and detailed documentation for the next phase.  Because the system requirements are accurately documented, major mistakes can be minimized.

| Fundamental Systems Development Strategies | | Systems Development Characteristics | | | | | |
|---|---|---|---|---|---|---|---|
| | | System Scale | System Uniqueness | Development Time Duration | Development Costs | System Test and Quality Assurance | Project Control of the organization |
| Systems Acquisition | Off-the-Shelf Package | Small to medium | Generic with little variation | Quick | Very Low | Producer or vendors | Simple |
| | ERP Systems | Medium to large | Generic with configuration and customization features | Short | Low | Producer or vendors | Vendor is usually involved |
| | SaaS | Typical application | Generic | Instant | Extremely Low | Service provider | Very simple |
| Systems Construction | | Vary | Unique | Long | High | Uncertain until the system runs for a time period | Complicated |
| Outsourcing | | Vary depending on the contract | Vary depending on the contract | Vary depending on the contract | Vary depending on the contract | Vary depending on contract | Low control |

Table 2.1. Comparison of Fundamental Systems Development Strategies

The major disadvantage of the waterfall approach is that the development process takes a long time to deliver the final new information system. This disadvantage can have a serious negative consequence in many cases when the systems requirements are significantly changed in response to the rapid changes of business environment during the development period, as the development process has to turn back to make needed changes though each of the affected phases. Generally, the waterfall approach is applied to large systems with clear and stable system requirements.

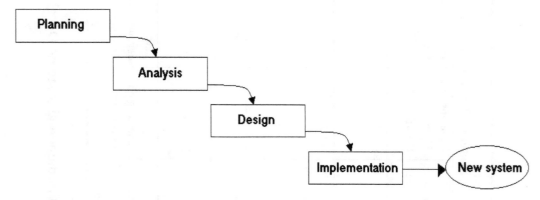

**Figure 2.4. Waterfall Approach to Constructing a New Information System**

### 2.4.2. Parallel approach

The **parallel approach** divides the system construction project into several subprojects that can be analyzed, designed, and implemented in parallel, as illustrated in Figure 2.5. The advantage of the parallel approach is that the project duration can be reduced significantly in comparison with the waterfall approach. The disadvantage of the parallel approach is that the subprojects are usually not independent and the complicated interrelationships between the subprojects often cause difficulties for the system integration.

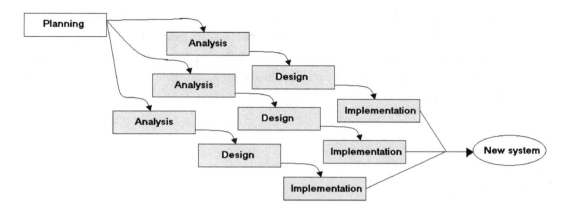

**Figure 2.5. Parallel Approach to Constructing a Large Information System**

### 2.4.3. Rapid application development (RAD) approach

The **rapid application development (RAD)** approach refers to a type of systems construction that uses minimal planning, analysis, and design in favor of rapid construction prototyping. Using the RAD approach, the planning, analysis, and design activities are interleaved with writing the software itself, and the documentations of planning, analysis, and design are reduced to virtually none. This allows system to be constructed much faster. More importantly, the RAD approach makes the construction process easy to respond to the system requirement changes, especially when the system requirements are vague until both the users and the software engineers understand the new system.

The main characteristics of the RAD approach are system **prototyping** and iterative construction process, as illustrated in Figure 2.6. A **system prototype** is a model product that represents main features of the target system, but is not an operational system. A prototype of the target system allows the users to provide comments and feedback with more specific requirements. This feedback is used for the software engineers to redesign and to re-construct the next prototype. The iterative development process carries on until the final new system is created.

The advantage of the RAD approach is a faster construction process. The disadvantage of the RAD approach is potential compromise of the quality of the final system because of the lack of methodical analysis, precise design, and formal documentations. In fact, it is rare to develop a large complex information system using the RAD approach.

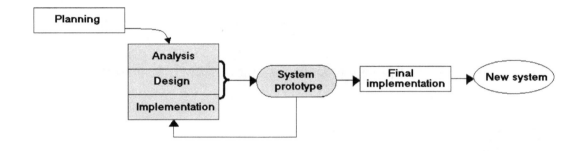

**Figure 2.6. Rapid Application Development (RAD) Approach**

### 2.4.4. Other variant approaches of RAP

In the software engineering field, there have been many variant approaches of RAD to constructing information systems. Each of these variant approaches has its unique characteristics. It is difficult to find a precise definition for each of them. **Extreme Programming (XP)** is a lightweight system construction approach. In the XP approach, the construction team is small (e.g., 2 to 12 people). The team keeps close interaction with the users to construct the small-scale system quickly. Coding of software is always performed by pairs of programmers to maintain the speed and the quality of construction. **Agile development** is a generalization of XP, but does not require pair programming. The construction team member might play multiple roles instead of the generic role of programming, which makes the interaction with the users more effective. In comparison with XP, agile development can be applied to larger information systems.

The **reuse-based development** approach emphasizes software reuse. The construction team searches for useable software parts in the software storage and makes modifications to fit the users' requirements quickly. Systematic software reuse is still the most promising strategy for increasing the productivity and improving the quality of systems development. Although the concept is simple, successful software reuse implementation is difficult in practice because of the dependence of reusable software on the context of applications.

### *Key Terms*

Systems development life cycle (SDLC)

Fundamental phases of SDLC

Planning phase

Analysis phase

Design phase

Implementation phase

Maintenance phase

Project sponsor

Project scope

Project scale

Risk of system development project

Risk assessment

Challenges for the information systems project management

Commercialized software products

ERP systems

Off-the-shelf software

Software as a service (SaaS)

Cloud computing

Three fundamental information systems development strategies

Systems acquisition

Systems construction

Outsourcing

Request for Proposal (RFP)

Comparison of the three systems development strategies

Waterfall approach of systems construction

Parallel approach of systems construction

Rapid application development (RA)

Prototyping

Agile development

Extreme programming (XP)

Reuse-based development

# CHAPTER 3. SYSTEMS PLANNING

The **systems planning phase** is the process of preliminary investigation to understand why a new information system should be created for the organization. It includes the following major steps.

(1) Initiating a system development project.

(2) Defining the scope of the new information system.

(3) Justifying of the feasibility.

(4) Scheduling the tasks.

(5) Assessing risks.

(6) Generating a system development project plan.


## 3.1. Initiating a System Development Project

A system development project is initiated by new business needs for information technology support. New business needs could occur when (1) the organization recognizes its problems of business process; (2) the organization explores new opportunities of information technology; or (3) the organization makes a proactive action in response to the business environment changes. New business needs could be conceived by either the top management of the organization, or the operational level of the organization, or the information systems professionals.

To formally initiate a new system development project, the project sponsor submits a document, called the **system request** to the organization for approval. The system request describes the considerations and the rationale of a new information system development project, and the development strategy (i.e., systems acquisition, or systems construction). The approval procedure follows the organizational policy and rules.

Once the system request is approved by the organization, a project planning team is formed to conduct a **feasibility study** for the system development project. A feasibility study includes three steps: defining the scope of the new information system, justifying the feasibility, and generating a system development project plan. The feasibility study is actually a preliminary system analysis without great details.

## 3.2. Defining the Scope of the New Information System

The first step of a feasibility study is to define the scope of the new information system in terms of the range of system requirements of the organization, the extent of the potential changes of business process of the organization, and constraints.

### 3.2.1. As-Is system

During the feasibility study, the as-is system for the system development project is described by the following aspects.

(1) What business processes will be affected by the development project, and what the current form of each of these business processes is.

(2) What stakeholders of the organization will be affected by the system development project, and how each of these stakeholders uses the current information system.

(3) What organizational units will be affected the system development project, and how each of these organizational units plays a part of the current information system.

### 3.2.2. To-Be system

The to-be system for the system development project is also described in the feasibility study by specifying the following aspects.

(1) What the form of each of the affected business processes will be.

(2) How each of the affected stakeholders uses the new information system.

(3) How each of the affected organizational units plays a part of the new information system.

### 3.2.3. Extent of the potential changes of the business process

The nature of a new information system is to change the business process of the organization to meet the organization's business needs by solving the problems in the current business process or taking the advantages of information technology to improve the business process.

The extent of the potential changes of business process can be categorized into business process automation (BPA), business process improvement (BPI), and business process reengineering (BPR), as discussed below.

### (1) *Business Process Automation (BPA)*

**BPA** is to automate manual processes by using computerized information systems. The major objective of a BPA project is to improve the efficiency of the business process in the organization. For instance, a small retail store currently processes the inventory manually. The manual process is not only slow, but also causes errors. A BPA project for this small business can fully automate the entire inventory process, including purchasing, receiving, adjusting, pricing, and selling. A BPA project has the following main characteristics.

● The process logics of the as-is system and the to-be system are similar except for that the to-be system is computerized. Thus, the changes to the organizational business process are minor.

● The risk of failure in a BPA project is low.

● The limitation of BPA is that the advantages of computerized information systems are underexplored.

### (2) *Business Process Improvement (BPI)*

**BPI** is to improve business processes which may or may not be computerized yet. The objective of a BPI project is to improve the organizational business process effectiveness (i.e., doing things in a right way) in addition to the efficiency (i.e., doing things fast). A BPI project could eliminate useless business processes, change the way of current process, or add new business processes to make the organizational business process more effective. BPI is a natural extension of BPA. Following the previous small retail store example, the BPA project can be expanded into a BPI project by including new business processes, say, inventory flow reporting and cash flow analysis for the store owner. In fact, BPI is always achievable for a BPA project through the use of information technology. A BPI project has the following main characteristics.

● There is a change to the current organizational business process. Useless processes will be eliminated, and new processes will be added to make the entire business process more effective.

● Because of the potential changes of the organizational business process, the risk of failure in a BPI project could be higher in comparison with a BPA project, especially when the potential changes are severe.

### (3) *Business Process Reengineering (BPR)*

**BPR** is to make radical changes to the current organizational business process, taking advantage of new ideas and information technologies. The rationale of BPR is that the fundamental way of the business operations is to be transformed entirely. Following the previous small retail store example, suppose the store owner decides to transform the brick-and-mortar business into an online retail store. The as-is system is no longer much relevant because the entire business process will never be the same. On the other hand, the to-be system seems to be unfamiliar to the store. A BPR project has the following main characteristics.

● The organizational business process will be changed radically. The current as-is system is not worth examination in detail. An extensive investigation of the to-be system is needed.

● Because of the radical changes of the organizational business process, the risk of failure in a BPR project is usually high.

### 3.3. Justifying the Feasibility

The next step of system planning is to identify the constraints and to justify the feasibility of the new information system project in three aspects: technological feasibility, economic feasibility, and organizational feasibility.

### 3.3.1. Constraints

A system development project is always subject to limited resources and special situations. The feasibility study team must identify the **constraints** of the organization on the new system project in the financial, organizational, and technological aspects, such as

- limited financial resources (budget);
- imperfect human resources competency of the organization;
- inadequate computing support facilities;
- the current platform of information system;
- insufficient physical facilities;
- possible conflicts caused by the project; and
- unresolved legal issues related to the new information system.

### 3.3.2. Technological feasibility

The justification of **technological feasibility** is to answer the question: "Is the technology ready for this project?" Specifically, the project planning team has to address the following two major factors.

(1) *The information system development strategy*

What is the strategy of systems development for this project? How long will this information system development project take? If the development strategy is systems acquisition, what potential candidate commercial software products are available on the market? How good are these commercial software products? If the development strategy is systems construction, what cutting-edge technology will be used for this project? Does the organization have the technological capacity to develop the new information system in-house?

(2) *System compatibility*

Would the current as-is system be compatible with the new to-be system in terms of hardware, networking, system infrastructure, data formats, and operational procedures? If not completely, what will be the difficulty in the migration from the current system to the new system?

### 3.3.3. Economic feasibility

Any new information system development project needs investment. The justification of **economic feasibility** is to answer the question: "Can we afford the project?" **Cost-benefit analysis** is the most commonly used method for evaluating the financial effectiveness of a new information system. The cost-benefit analysis procedure is to determine the benefits and savings that are expected from the new information system and to compare them with the costs. The project can be justified only if the estimated benefits outweigh the costs.

The difficult part of a cost-benefit analysis is the estimation of costs and benefits. Generally, a new information system can have **tangible costs** and **intangible costs**. Tangible costs are visible and can be easily measured in the monetary term. The estimation of tangible costs is relatively straightforward. Applying the concepts of accounting, the costs of an information system development project include **development costs** and **operational costs**. Development costs are the expenses for the creation of the new system, such as expenses for purchasing new hardware and software, salaries of project team members or consultant fees, and other one-time investment on making the new system. Operational costs are the expenses for day-to-day operations of the new system, such as software annual licensing fees, monthly network provider fees, hardware upgrades and repair charges, salaries of operational personnel, and other expenses to keep the new system ongoing. Intangible costs are relatively invisible and are difficult to measure. For example, the new system has risks of failure, and the costs caused by a possible failure are difficult to estimate.

The estimation of benefits of the new system is generally difficult, especially when the scope of the new system is large and BPI or BPR is involved. A new information system can have **tangible benefits** and **intangible benefits**. Tangible benefits are the investment returns that are visible and can be easily measured in the monetary term. Examples of tangible benefits are:
● manpower saving as a result of process automation;
● lower inventory costs as a result of better inventory control; and
● sales increase as a result of reducing back orders.

Intangible benefits are less visible and are difficult to be measured in the monetary term explicitly. For instance, the new information system will make the alliance with the business strategic partners stronger. This benefit is a long term effect of the new system, and is difficult to be measured explicitly. Examples of intangible benefits are:

- improved relations with business partners;
- improved customer services;
- improved company's image; and
- complying with the government or industrial regulations.

To document the cost-benefit analysis, the project planning team needs to present the cost-benefit analysis result in spreadsheet, as shown by an example in Figure 3.1.

A cost-benefit analysis applies several methods because any single method has its limitations, as explained below.

(1) **Cash flow method** - The cash flow method shows the projection of the estimated costs and benefits that are related to the new information system over the next three to five years. Commonly, **present values** are used to measure the cash flows (see the formula of the highlighted cell in Figure 3.1). The analyst estimates the interest rate (or inflation rate) for each year based on assumptions. The cash flow method shows detailed cash flows, but does not show the overall financial consequence of the project.

(2) **Return on investment method** - The return on investment (ROI) method measures the average rate of the return on the total investment over the next several years. The ROI method shows whether the project is worth, but does not show whether the organization has enough cash flows to support the project.

(3) **Break-even point method** - The break-even point method determines when the organization fully recovers its investment on the project. In the context of information systems project, the concept of break-even point is depicted in Figure

3.2. The break-even point shows the financial risk of the project, but might be biased against a project with great long-term benefits.

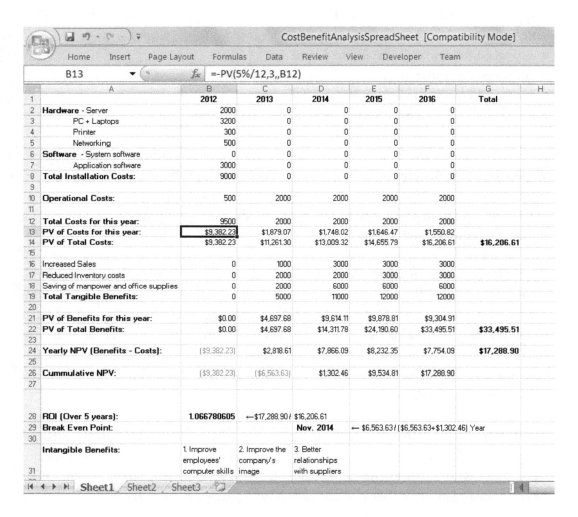

**Figure 3.1. Spreadsheet for Cost-Benefit Analysis**

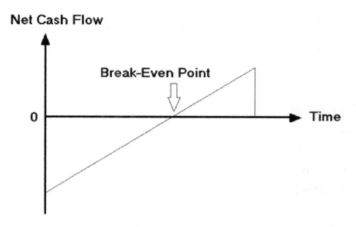

**Figure 3.2. The Break-Even Point Method**

In fact, **budgeting** for a project is based on a cost-benefit analysis. Also, cost-benefit analyses should be conducted across the entire system life cycle to continuously assess the value of the project as well as the actual performance of the new information system. The systems analysis phase and the post-project assessment in the systems maintenance phase must provide their independent cost-benefit analysis reports that will test the accuracy of the cost-benefit analysis of the systems planning phase.

### 3.3.4. Organizational feasibility

The justification of **organizational feasibility** is to answer the question: "Would people like the new system?" Here, people include the stakeholders of the organization, the stockholders of the organization, the managers at all levels, and the users of the system. Along with the global proliferation of information technology and the overall enhancement of computer literacy, resistance against new information systems has been diminished over the past years in general. Nevertheless, the project planning team must assess possible resistance through surveys and/or interviews.

## 3.4. Scheduling the Project Activities

The project planning team needs to identify the activities that are involved in the project. Each activity has its attributes including:

- name of the activity;
- definition of the activity;
- duration of the activity;
- prerequisite activity of the activity;
- starting time and finishing time of the activity; and
- responsible personnel of the activity.

The identified activities of the project are displayed in a **Gantt chart** (see an example in Figure 3.3) for the project control.

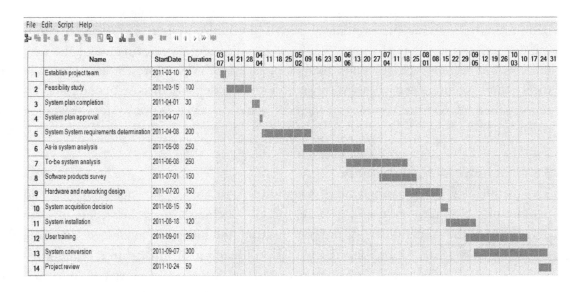

**Figure 3.3. Gantt Chart for Project Management**

## 3.5. Assessing Risks

The project planning team needs to recognize potential risk factors and address how the project team can eliminate the sources of risk before they threaten the project. Common factors of **risk** in information systems projects are:

- overly optimistic schedule;
- underestimated budget;
- high turnover rate of project team members;
- unstable vendors; and
- volatile business environment.

## 3.6. Generating System Development Project Plan

In the final stage of systems planning, the project planning team edits a system development project plan. The **project plan** is submitted to the organization for approval. Again, the approval procedure follows the organizational policy and rules. The project plan usually includes the following components for the system development project.

- Scope of the new system.
- Feasibility study results.
- Schedule of project activities.
- Risk assessment.
- Budget and other resource needs.

The approved system development project plan provides the guideline for the systems analysis phase as well as the entire system development process.

## *Key Terms*

Systems planning
Initiating system development project
System request

Scope of the new information system
Feasibility study
As-is system

To-be system

Business process automation (BPA)

Business process improvement (BPI)

Business process reengineering (BPR)

Constraints

Technological feasibility

Economic feasibility

Organizational feasibility

Cost-benefit analysis

Tangible costs

Intangible costs

Tangible benefits

Intangible benefits

Development costs

Operational costs

Project activities

Gantt chart

Risk

Project plan

## *Exercises of Systems Analysis and Design Course Project*

1. Meet your group members to identify a business organization which is going to use information technology to improve its business processes. Small business is ideal. A department of a medium-sized organization is also feasible. One or more group members must be familiar with the business firm so that the systems requirement analysis would not heavily rely on interviews.

2. Discuss the scope of your project in terms of the business process you are going to investigate.

3. Identify the problems of the current business process, and opportunities of improvement.

4. Describe the as-is system of the organization.

5. Discuss your vision of the to-be system for the organization. Identify the components of BPA and BPI for the business process.

6. Discuss the feasibilities for the organization to implement the to-be system.

7. Discuss the constraints of the organization for the to-be system

# CHAPTER 4. SYSTEMS ANALYSIS

The central task of the **systems analysis phase** is to determine the requirements for the new information system. The major steps of the systems analysis phase include

(1) Collecting information for understanding the system requirements.

(2) Specifying the system requirements using business process modeling techniques.

(3) Contrasting the as-is system and the to-be system in terms of system requirements.

(4) Documenting the system requirements for the systems design phase.

## 4.1. System Requirements

A **system requirement** is a statement or expression that specifies what the information system must perform or what characteristics the information system must have. The central task of systems analysis phase is to determine the system requirements for the system development.

There are two types of system requirements: functional requirements and non-functional requirements, as explained next.

### 4.1.1. Functional requirements

A **functional requirement** specifies what the information system must do to accomplish the business processes, the information provision, and the business rules of the organization.

### (1) **Business process**

The business processes implemented by the information system are the major concern for the organization. In fact, the terms "business process", "business operation", "business function", "business scenario", "task", and "use case" have not been rigorously differentiated, but are exchangeable in the systems analysis and design field. The term **business process** is adopted in this textbook because it is more commonly used than others in business. In general, a business process is a set of business activities performed by human actors and/or the information system to accomplish a specific outcome. In the view of the system approach, a business process is a hierarchy of sub-processes, as illustrated in Figure 4.1.

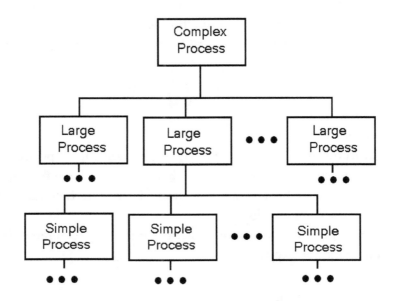

**Figure 4.1. Hierarchy of Business Process**

## (2) **User-perceived information**

User-perceived information is considered to be the central components of functional requirements and is the major measure of the effectiveness of information system. Here, the terms **data** and **information** are interchangeable; that is, they can be either raw facts or the processed evidences for business activities. A piece of user-perceived information is always associated with a business process. Conceptually, there are three basic types of user-perceived information: input, output, and navigation information.

- **Input** is the acquired information captured by the business process.
- **Output** is the delivered information produced by the business process.

- **Navigation information** provides the directions for the user to proceed through the business process.

### (3) Business rules

A **business rule** is a statement that aims to influence or guide business processes in the organization. A business rule specifies the relationships between an anticipated condition and the expected actions or outcomes. Using information systems, business rules are implemented through coded software. For the time being, there is a lack of systematic techniques for mapping the business rules and the information system onto each other. As the perspectives of business rules are crucial for the systems acquisition development, the system analysts must investigate important business rules of the organization that are supposed to be implemented in the information system.

### 4.1.2. Nonfunctional requirements

A **nonfunctional requirement** specifies a characteristic or property of the information system must have. The major types of nonfunctional requirements are discussed below.

### (1) Usability requirements

**Usability** requirements specify the user-friendliness of the information system, such as

- quality of the user interface of the system, and the easiness of use;
- degree of error tolerance;
- quality of documentation, including **reference documents**, **operation manuals**, and **tutorials**; and
- unique operational features, e.g., data visualization.

### (2) Security

Security requirements specify the safety issues of the information system. The system should have safeguards against unauthorized access, cyber attacks, and information loss.

### (3) **Vendor**

Vendor requirements specify the characters of the vendors who are the potential providers of the hardware, the networks, and the software products for the information system, such as

- reputation;
- services (e.g., maintenance and upgrading);
- business alliance for the long term consideration;
- training availability; and
- standardization and industrial common platform.

### (4) **Performance**

Performance requirements specify the quality of operation of the information system, such as

- reliability - the extent to which the system is available to the users in all circumstances;
- **scalability** - the ability of the system to increase the capacity in response to additional needs; and
- speed - the time used for business process.

### (5) Others

Unlike functional requirements which are more or less certain as a result of business process modeling, nonfunctional requirements can include many other factors which may or may not be concerns in general, such as:

- multiple languages;
- pricing competitiveness;
- licensing / leasing options; and
- cultural and religion consideration.

## 4.2. Techniques of Requirements Information Collection

To determine the system requirements for the new information system, the system analysts need to collect as much information as possible to understand the organization's requirements. The requirements information collecting process documents the system requirements, and lays the foundation for the systems analysis phase. There are many techniques that can be used for collecting requirements information, and each of these techniques has its pros and cons as discussed below.

### 4.2.1. Experiencing and observation

The systems analysts should possess certain knowledge of the business processes in general. To effectively analyze the organization's specific business processes, it is ideal for the systems analysts to have **first-hand experiences** of the pertinent business processes as the user of the information system in that organization, so that they can understand more about the problems of the as-is system and opportunities for the to-be system. The downside of experiencing is that personal experiences are always of a limited scope and could be biased.

**Observation** is the act of watching ongoing business processes. Observation is close to first-hand experiencing, and can reach a wide scope within a short time period in comparison with experiencing. However, observation is still time consuming. Observing all business processes in a large information system is impossible. Also, observation might violate rules in many organizations.

### 4.2.2. Interview

**Interview** is the most commonly used technique for collecting requirements information. It can reach a wide range of the users of the information system including managers, operational staff, and customers. Interviews can be conducted on the one-to-one basis or on a group basis. The typical steps of interview process are discussed below.

### (1) Designing interview questions

To understand the system requirements, the systems analysts need to design interview questions that can reveal the sought information at the greatest extent.

The interview questions could require specific answers, or could be open to the interviewees for unspecific answers.

## (2) **Selecting interviewees**

The direct users of the information system in the different positions of the organization are the primary group of interviewees. Other stakeholders who may not be the direct users of the system can also be candidate interviewees. Clearly, the selected interviewees must be the best knowledgeable people in the organization to answer the interview questions.

## (3) **Conducting interview**

It is recommended to send interview questions to the interviewee before the interview. The interview act must comply with the rules and norms of the organization. Recording may be applied, but is unnecessary for systems analysis and design in general. As the systems analysis is usually not an emergent matter, the interviewer should not interrupt the interviewee's speech, should give enough time for the interviewee to think, and should friendly answer the interviewee's relevant questions.

## (4) **Verifying and releasing interview findings**

After an interview, the interviewer compiles the interview results. If the systems analysts are unsure about the accuracy of the interview results, they should send the compiled results back to the interviewee to verify the interview results. All interview results are documented and summarized at the end of the interview session. The documented interview results should be released without attaching any interviewee's name and be available for the organization.

An interview may or may not be face-to-face, and can be conducted through teleconferencing. Interviews are very expensive if the times spent on the interviews are counted. Also, interviews may not always go as planned, because the information system development may not be the top working agenda of the interviewees.

### 4.2.3. Joint Analytical Development (JAD)

**Joint Analytical Development (JAD)** is a team-based requirements information collection technique. The objective of JAD is to bring representatives of all stakeholders of the organization together, including the project development team, the users in all relevant departments, and the management, to identify system requirements for the development. JAD has a long history in the IT field, and has been widely used in the industry.

The form of JAD varies depending on the organization structure and the use of modern technology for knowledge sharing. The entire JAD process has several sessions. Each session is a well structured meeting with a clear objective, and is facilitated by a facilitator. The facilitator could be the system development project team leader, or an IT consultant with experiences and skills in JAD.

### 4.2.4. Documents review

A **documents review** is to analyze the documentation of the current as-is system, including the systems analysis and design reports for the as-is system as well as the operational and maintenance records, to understand the requirements for the to-be system. Realistically, many information systems are not well documented. Also, the documents for the as-is system may not be particularly relevant to the to-be system.

### 4.2.5. Questionnaire

A **questionnaire** is a survey instrument that consists of a series of written questions for collecting information from respondents. Similar to the interview and JAD techniques, the selection of participants for survey is important. The direct users of the information system in the different positions of the organization are the primary candidate participants. Other stakeholders who may not be the direct users of the system can also be candidate participants. The candidate participants must possess the best knowledge on the questions.

Many questionnaire design techniques are available to ensure the quality of survey. For example, to validate the answers to questions, the same multiple-choice question could be listed more than once with different choice orders.

The questionnaire technique has advantages of low cost over other requirement information collection techniques. However, a long list of questions may frustrate the participants. The responses rates of questionnaires are usually low. A low response rate can result in sampling bias.

### 4.2.6. Selecting techniques for collecting requirements information

As discussed in the above sub-sections, each of the information collection techniques has its strengths as well as weaknesses. Accordingly, more than often, the systems analysts must select several techniques, given the fact that none of these techniques is perfect for systems analysis and design. The system development team selects the most suitable techniques to ensure that all functional requirements and nonfunctional requirements for the to-be system are complete, unbiased, and accurate.

### 4.3. Business Process Modeling

The information collected for the system requirements determination through the information collection is usually narrative, unstructured, and disconnected. To synthesize and formalize all information collected using scientific terms, **systems modeling** techniques must be applied.

As pointed out in Chapter 1, systems analysis and design engage many areas of information systems, including database, networking, programming, hardware and operating systems. Accordingly, systems analysis and design involve many systems modeling subjects such as data models, programming models, network models, etc. However, **business process modeling** is the primary systems modeling task for systems analysis and design because the **business process model** of the organization is the central abstraction that describes the business functional requirements and lays the foundation for other systems models for the system development.

In business process modeling, a **business process** is a collection of related and structured activities or tasks that produce a specific output(s) in response to an input(s). In the systems analysis and design context, the term business process refers to an information process, but not a physical process (e.g., Cooking). There are three main types of business processes: management process, operational process, and supporting process. A **management process** is a managerial decision making process, such as budgeting and supplier selection. An **operational process** is a business process of routine business operations. The operation processes constitute the core business and create the primary value stream for the organization. Typical examples of operational process are purchasing, ordering, and payment. A **supporting process** is a business process that supports management processes and operational processes. Examples of supporting process are bookkeeping and banking. Clearly, the cut-line between the three types of business processes can never be sharp. Generally, automating the operational processes is the target of BPA, and improving the management processes and the supporting processes is the target of BPI.

A **business process model** is a model that defines the way in which the business processes are carried out to accomplish the intended goal of the entire system at multiple abstraction levels.

## 4.4. Major Tools of Business Process Modeling

A **business process modeling tool** is a **formalized visual language** that provides systems analysts with the ability to describe the business processes unambiguously, to visualize the business processes for systematic understanding, and to communicate the business process models for the information systems development. Natural languages (e.g., English) are incapable to model complex business process. Diagrams (graphics) have been used as tools for business process modeling in the information systems field. There have been many types of business process modeling tools, and each of them has its own style and syntax to serve its particular purpose. The most commonly used business process modeling tools are Data Flow Diagram (DFD), the Unified Modeling Language (UML), and Business Process Modeling Notation (BPMN).

### 4.4.1. Data Flow Diagram (DFD)

A **data flow diagram** (**DFD**) is a graphical representation of the business processes and the flows of data through an information system. The DFD tool was developed in the 1970s and has served as a foundation of other business process tools. There have been a few variants of notations to draw DFDs, but they symbolize the same meanings. In this textbook, we use the Gane and Sarson style.

The central concept of DFD is a **top-down approach** to understanding a system. It is essentially the breaking down of a system progressively to gain insight into its compositional sub-systems. Using the top-down approach, an overview of the system is formulated. The overall system is then described in detail by its subsystems. Each subsystem is in turn viewed as a system, and then refined in yet greater detail. The refining process continues until the entire specification is reduced to basic elements. This refining process is called **decomposition**. In the course of decomposition a set of hierarchical DFDs are obtained, and the business processes and their input and output data are clearly defined.

The top-down approach is consistent with the system concept that views a system in a holistic manner and concerns an understanding of a system by examining the components and their interactions within the system.

Using DFDs, systems analysts are able to visualize and communicate how the information system operates and what the information system will accomplish. For instance, the DFDs of the to-be system and the DFDs of the as-is system can be compared to show the differences between the two systems in the aspects of BPA and BPI.

The DFD tool is good at modeling business processes in describing processes and data. However, the DFD tool has its weakness in describing business rules. For example, exact timing and conditions of process sequences are not displayed in DFDs explicitly.

### 4.4.2. Unified Modeling Language (UML)

The Unified Modeling Language (UML) is a general-purpose modeling tool in the field of software engineering for constructing all types of computerized systems including computer operating systems, industrial control systems, geographical information systems, image processing systems, data communication systems, business information systems, and others. Business process modeling is just one of its applications of the UML. The UML was developed in the 1990s in response to the movement of object-oriented programming and object-oriented systems analysis and design. The objective of the UML is to provide a common vocabulary of object-oriented terms and diagramming techniques for object-oriented systems development. The object-oriented approach views a system as a collection of self-contained objects, including both data and processes. The UML includes a set of various types of diagrams with different subjects of modeling and diversified graphics styles. Generally, the UML diagrams can be categorized into two major groups: structure diagrams for representing data and static relationships and behavior diagrams for representing dynamic relationships among the objects. Four dominant UML diagramming techniques are:

● use case diagrams,
● class diagrams,
● sequence diagrams, and
● behavior state machine diagrams.

As the UML is a set of several different modeling tools, learning and using the UML are not easy. Diversified diagrams in the UML can provide detailed specifications for software engineering in many perspectives, and thus are ideal for systems construction. However, the UML is weak in the aspect of top-down system modeling, and is not a favorable tool for systems acquisition development.

### 4.4.3. Business Process Modeling Notations (BPMN)

Business Process Modeling Notation (BPMN) is a graphical representation for specifying the sequences and steps of business processes. BPMN was developed in the 1990s. It is based on the traditional flowcharting technique. The objective of BPMN is to support business process modeling by providing intuitive notations for complex business rules. BPMN is intended to serve as a tool to bridge the communication gap that frequently occurs between the business process design phase and the implementation phase.

The flowchart style diagrams in BPMN can provide detailed specifications for automation of business processes, and thus are ideal for systems construction. However, BPMN is short of the ability of top-down system modeling, and is not an ideal tool for systems acquisition development.

### 4.4.4. Summary of business process modeling tools

Traditionally, the information technology industry has been focusing on the modeling tools for construction specifications for software engineering, and the UML is a typical example of this reality. These tools are designed to describe the deep structures and system components for software construction, but are not meant for software feature descriptions. Consumers of commercialized business application software products would like to have explicit specifications about the business process that can be carried out by the software products, rather than the specifications for the construction of the software product. This is similar to the fact that consumers of cars never want to review the engineers' manufacturing blueprints in making their purchase decisions. Since nowadays there is no commonly applied format of business software specifications that can be used for conveying the software features to consumers, sellers of commercialized business software products use free-format descriptions and *ad hoc* style demos to market their software products. Software consumers have few specific guidelines for the examination of utilities of software products, but use their highly subjective judgments based on thorough reviews of the software products based on the available demos, documents, and customers' evaluations.

To facilitate the systems acquisition development, the business process modeling tool must warrant that its modeling results can be effectively used for examinations of software products. As discussed in the previous sub-sections, DFD is a practicably workable tool for systems acquisition development in comparison with other builder-centered business process modeling tools. More importantly, once you have learned one typical modeling tool, you have developed the ability to learn other modeling tools quickly.

## 4.5. Data Flow Diagram

### 4.5.1. Overview of DFD

A DFD shows the concerned business processes, their inputs and outputs data, the users of the data, and the storages of data. Figure 4.2 shows an example of DFD that models a part of the advertising job order process of an advertising agency. Before discussing details about the DFD method, we take a glance on this example.

The DFD in Figure 4.2 seems to represent the processes of client service. Usually, people start reading or drawing a DFD from its upper-left corner. The following system functional requirements can be perceived from the DFD.

• The first symbol on the left side of the DFD in Figure 4.2 represents "Client" who sends inquiries, advertising job orders, and requests for changes to job orders to the advertising agency.

• The client service makes several actions (or processes) in response to the client's inputs, including recording the client data for an initial contact, processing and answering client inquiries, and filing changes to the existing advertising order.

• The cline service also files advertising job order for the client, and sends the order to another process called "Job Scheduling".

• The client service has the responsibility to inform the client once the advertising job order has been scheduled.

• Two data stores are used for the client service: "Client Data" and "Job Schedules".

• There are many data flows in the client service. These data flows symbolize the inputs of the client to the system, the outputs of the client service to the client, as well as the data flows within the entire client service process.

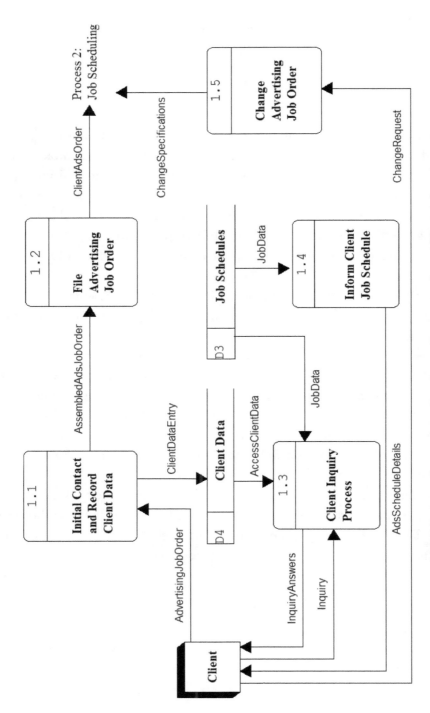

**Figure 4.2. DFD for a Part of the Business Process of an Advertising Agency**

Several important properties of DFD you can learn from this simple example.

● DFD is a much better tool than the natural languages (e.g., English) for describing information systems requirements. A DFD contains rich information about system requirements, and is precise in comparison with narrative descriptions.

● DFD is quite simple to use, and is easy to understand.

● The processes expressed in a DFD (e.g., "Initial Contact and Record Client Data", "Client Inquiry Process", "Inform Client Job Schedule", etc. in Figure 4.2) may or may not operate sequentially. Realistically, major aggregate business processes operate in a parallel manner. Only simple business processes are carried out in the sequential manner. This property makes the DFD method more usable for business process modeling in comparison with process flow chart methods which are deficient of modeling parallel business processes.

● This example of DFD represents a simple business process. If the business process is complicated, a one-page DFD can be huge. A huge DFD is not practically usable for communicating system requirements. This reality is similar to the fact that few people use a huge one-page map for extensive global travels. Actually, the DFD method can solve this problem by itself. We will discuss this issue later in this section.

DFD has only four elements: external entity, process, data store, and data flow.

## (1) **External entity**

An **external entity** is a class of persons (e.g., Client) or a class of organizations (e.g., Suppliers) outside the system. An external entity provides the source of data for the system and/or receives the data from the system. The name of an external entity is a unique **noun**.

Any **internal entity** who is an actor within the system never appears in DFD. For instance, in Figure 4.2, the clerk who processes the data of Client does not appear in the DFD because the clerk is actually a part of the processor of the information system. In many cases, an entity can be both internal and external. For instance, if managers receive managerial reports from the system, the class of these managers (e.g., Manager) is an external entity of the system. These managers can also play roles of an internal entity which is not modeled in the DFD.

## (2) **Process**

A **process** is set of business activities (e.g., Order Process) of the system. It processes the input and produces the output. Conceptually, a process can be manual or computerized. The name of a process is a unique **verb** or **verb phrase**. Each process has its unique identification number (ID). The value of ID is not important, but indicates the level of the process as explained later in this chapter.

The identification of processes is rather subjective in comparison with the identification of other elements of DFD, because there is no rule for grouping business activities. As discussed later in this chapter, this is not a critical problem for using DFD for business process modeling, because a complex process can be decomposed level-by-level into **primitive processes** which are reasonably objective.

## (3) **Data store**

A **data store** is a data repository of a set of integrated data used by the system. It can be a data file (e.g., Client File), a data table or a set of closely correlated data tables of database (Inventory and Sales Data). Conceptually, a data store can be a booklet or a file cabinet in manual systems, and can be digitalized in computerized systems. A data store has a unique **noun**, and a unique identification number (ID). The value of ID is not important.

A data store should represent meaningfully integrated data items. For instance, "Client Data" is better than "Client Names" for a data store. On the other hand, a data store should not represent vaguely aggregate data such as "Advertising Database".

## (4) **Data flow**

A **data flow** is an instance of data item (e.g., client name) or a set of data (e.g., client profile) that flows from its source to its destination. A data flow can flow between an external entity and a process, or between two processes, or between a process and a data store. The name of a data flow is a unique **noun**. A data flow is one-way flow. Data flows represent the inputs and outputs of processes in DFD. There are several tips in making data flows.

- There is no data flow between two external entities because any data flow that bypasses a process actually bypasses the concerned system.
- There is no data flow between two data stores because it makes little sense to move stored data around without processing.
- There is no data flow between an external entity and a data store because any external entity is not allowed to access the system unless a process of the system is involved.
- A process has at least one input data flow and at least one output data flow.

Note that in information systems analysis and design no physical goods flow is considered in the business process modeling. A physical goods flow that is relevant to the information system must have its companion data flow for information processing. For example, a physical flow named "Delivered appliance" would make no sense to the information system, but a data flow named "Appliance delivery slip" could be applied to the business process in DFD.

The DFD elements and explanations are summarized in Figure 4.3.

## 4.5.2. Systems thinking approach

A **system** is a set of interacting or interdependent components that form an integrated whole to achieve a certain goal. An information system is a system. From the viewpoint of systems analysis, a computerized information system is an organized set of computerized business processes and the data in their specific forms to provide the users with information services.

**Systems thinking** is the process of understanding how the components of the system influence one another within a whole. Systems thinking has been defined as an effective approach to systems analysis. It provides a view of the business process as a whole in the context of information services, and concerns an understanding of the linkages and interactions between the elements that compose the entirety of the information system.

| DFD Elements | Symbols | Explanations |
|---|---|---|
| **External Entity** |  Name | An **external entity** is a class of persons or a class of organizations outside the system. It provides the source of data for the system and/or receives the data from the system. The name of an external entity is a unique **noun**. |
| **Process** | 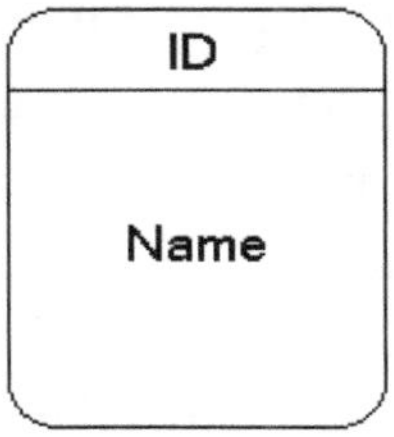 ID<br>Name | A **process** is set of business activities of the system. It processes the input and produces the output. The name of a process is a unique **verb** or **verb phrase**. Each process has its unique identification number (ID). The value of ID is not important, but indicates the level of the process. |
| **Data Store** |  ID Name | A **data store** is a data repository of a set of integrated data used by the system. It can be a data file, a data table, or a set of data tables. A data store has a unique **noun**, and a unique identification number (ID). The value of ID is not important. |
| **Data Flow** | 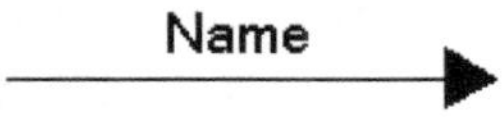 Name → | A **data flow** is an instance of data item or a set of data that flows between an external entity and process, or between two processes, or between a process and a data store. The name of a data flow is a unique **noun**. |

**Figure 4.3. DFD Elements**

An information system has two important common characteristics of system: an information system has its overall goal of information services (see Figure 4.4), and an information system has its structure defined by the components and their composition. To understand the components and their interaction relationships of a complex information system, one must **decompose** the entire system into **sub-systems**. If a sub-system is still a complex system, it is decomposed further. The decomposition process continues until all components of the entire system and their compositional structure describe the perceptible and measureable system requirements. This approach to systems thinking is called a **top-down approach**, which is illustrated in Figure 4.5.

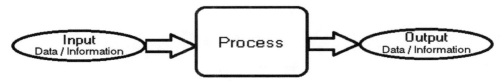

**Figure 4.4. Systems Thinking: Information System Entirety**

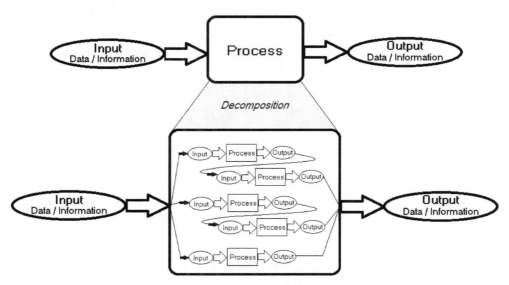

**Figure 4.5. Systems Thinking Approach to Information Systems Analysis**

In fact, the top-down systems thinking and system decomposition process can be observed ubiquitously in the day-to-day life. Map zoom-in is a typical example of top-down system decomposition (see Figure 4.6). The top level map provides the overall territory. To locate where the traveler would like to reach, she must zoom-in the map progressively to find the perceptible and measureable site.

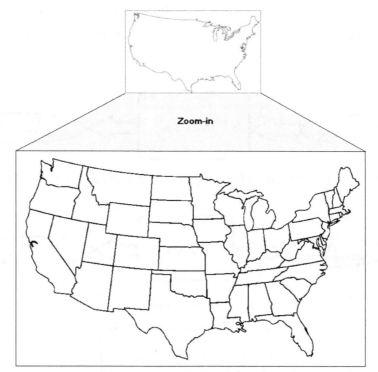

**Figure 4.6. System Thinking in Day-to-Day Life: Map Zoom-in**

### 4.5.3. Context diagram

It is common to draw a context-level data flow diagram first, which shows the interaction between the system and the external entities which act as data sources and data destinations of the system. A **context diagram** is also commonly known as "**Level-0 DFD**". A context diagram shows the entire system as a single process, and represents the system's interactions with the environment (i.e., external entities) using data flows.

Figure 4.7 is an example of context diagram. The context diagram describes the overall context of the information system of an advertising agency as follows.

• The system serves the clients by processing their advertising job orders.

• The system deals with printing companies and radio stations to fulfill the advertising jobs requested by the clients.

• The system provides advertisement designs to the printing companies and transcripts to the radio stations for the advertising jobs.

• The system also processes various types of invoices and payments in running the business.

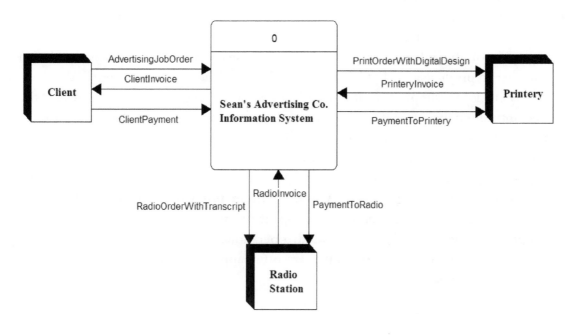

**Figure 4.7. Context Diagram**

The context diagram in Figure 4.7 represents shows the following characteristics of context diagram.

(1) A context diagram has a single overall process that represents the entire information system.

(2) A context diagram includes all external entities.

(3) A context diagram includes all major data flows that represent the substantial interactions with the external entities.

(4) A context diagram does not show data stores which are inside the overall process.

### 4.5.4. Decomposition

The context diagram of an information system represents the overall system but does not describe the perceptible and measurable system requirements in detail for the system design. To understand more about the information system, the system analysts must decompose the entire information system into sub-systems. To do so, the system analysts identify **segments** of the system. A DFD segment represents one part of the information system. All the segments are eventually combined together to produce a DFD that shows the details of the system to a certain degree.

There is no simple rule for the identification of segments. Nevertheless, the decomposition begins with the context diagram, and is to visualize the business processes within the system. As discussed earlier in this chapter, there are three main types of business processes: operational process, management process, and supporting process. An **operational process** is a business process of routine business operations (e.g., sales). A **management process** is a managerial decision making process (e.g., scheduling). A **supporting process** is a business process that supports management processes and operational processes (e.g., accounting). Accordingly, the following **heuristics** are often applied to identify segments for the system decomposition.

**(1) Starting with the external entities.**

*Heuristic-1:* *For each external entity, there is a segment which contains an operation process(es) and/or a support process(s) to provide information services to the external entity.*

Following this heuristic, three segments for the three external entities are identified as shown in Figure 4.8 through Figure 4.10.

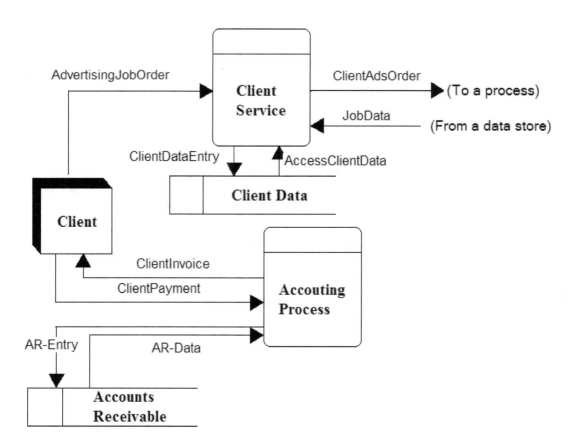

**Figure 4.8. A Segment for the Client Entity of the System in Figure 4.7.**

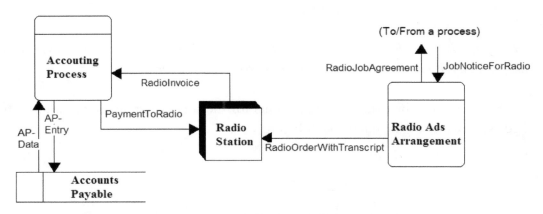

**Figure 4.9. A Segment for the Radio Entity of the System in Figure 4.7.**

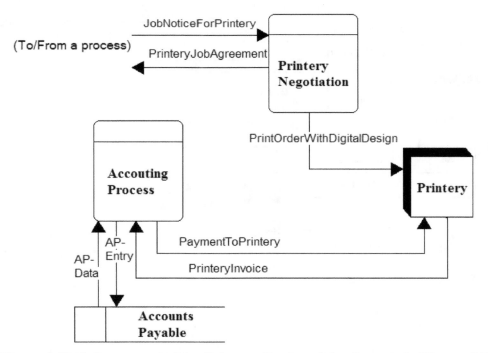

**Figure 4.10. A Segment for the Printery Entity of the System in Figure 4.7.**

(2) **Analyzing organizational support**.

*Heuristic-2*: *For each function areas (or department) of the organization, including accounting, human resource management, marketing, finance, sales management, and supplier chain management, identify a segment(s) with a general supporting process(es) that supports the processes in the identified segments for external entities.*

In this example of small system, only accounting supporting process is applicable. Figure 4.11 shows the segment with the accounting supporting process. Apparently, this segment has heavy overlaps with the segments for external entities. This is not a problem for this stage of segments identification.

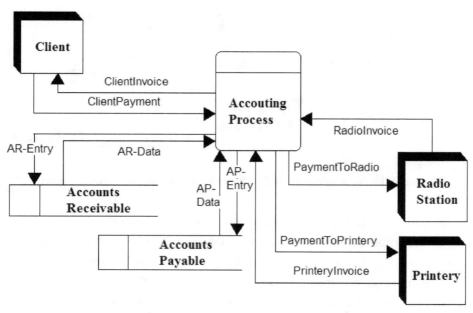

**Figure 4.11. A Segment of the Accounting Functional Area**

**(3) Analyzing managerial decisions.**

*Heuristic-3:* *Look into managerial decision processes that are applicable to the systems.*

In this example, job scheduling is a routine managerial decision making process that is applicable to this system. Figure 4.12 shows the segment with the Job Scheduling process. The segment shown in Figure 4.12 includes data flows that are shown in other segments. This is not a problem. In fact, the overlaps between the identified segments are useful for the integration of the segments.

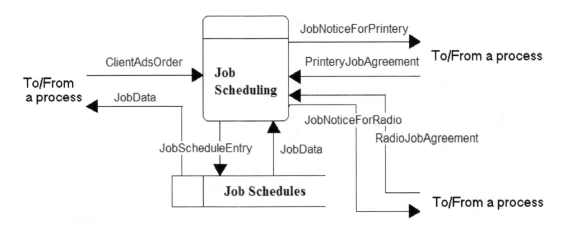

**Figure 4.12. A Segment of Managerial Decisions - Scheduling**

Several important points for decomposition are worth noting.
(1) System decomposition needs business skills and system thinking skills. The systems analysts need to be familiar with the three types of business processes in the business organization in order to identify segments for the information system. They must also have the system perspective of the information system in order to decompose the entire system.

(2) The decomposition procedure is rather artistic. The identification of segments highly depends on the system analyst's view of the business processes. In other

words, the same system can be decomposed in many different ways. This is similar to the case of map zooming that each map system has its unique way of zooming a map. Theoretically, this is not a considerable problem for a systems analysis using DFD, because a system can eventually be decomposed into primitive processes which can be clearly defined regardless of how the system is decomposed. Practically, business people (including systems analysts) often share the common understanding of business processes in general. For example, in our example, the concepts of Accounting Process for Accounts Payable and Accounts Receivable processes and Job Scheduling Process are quite straightforward in the business world.

(3) To describe the segments clearly, one step of decomposition creates around 7 (plus or minus 2) segments in common practices. This makes it possible to present the integrated segments on one print page for visualization. More importantly, the decomposition progression provides the system analysts with great detail information of the system requirements.

(4) The identified segments overlap each other as a result of having the same data flows, data stores, or oven processes. This would make the integration of segments easier.

### 4.5.5. Level-1 diagram

Once all segments of the entire system have been identified, the system analysis team integrates these segments into one DFD which is called the **Level-1 DFD**. A business process model has one, and only one, Level-1 DFD. Clearly, the integration eliminates the overlaps between the segments, and may add more connections between the segments to present the system as a whole.

The Level 1 DFD shows how the system is divided into sub-systems (or processes). A process deals with an external entity through data flows, or provides business supporting functions, or supports managerial decision making. The Level-1 DFD also identifies internal data stores that are used by the system to carry out the processes. It also shows the data flows between the various parts of the system. Figure 4.13 is the Level-1 DFD for the system represented in Figure 4.7.

The general properties of DFD can be fully observed in the Level-1 DFD.

- Each process, data store, data flow, and external entity has a unique name.
- Assign IDs to the processes and the data stores. The values of the IDs are not important.
- The layout of DFD is not crucial. In other words, it does not matter where the DFD elements are placed. However, the number of data flows that cross each other should be minimized to avoid confusion or disorganization. Commonly, the shared data stores are placed in the middle of the diagram, the external entities are placed near the edges, and the processes are placed close to the data stores. If necessary, data stores and external entities can be duplicated.
- Generally, the processes represented in a Level-1 DFD operate in a parallel manner, and a sequential order between the processes may or may not exist.

Clearly, drawing a correct and communicative DFD is a challenging job. It is not unusual that a DFD is drafted for many times.

### 4.5.6. Balancing

The decomposition of a Level-1 DFDs can go further into Level-2, Level-3, as so on, as shown in the next sub-sections. Because of the top-down nature of decomposition, it is a convention in the systems analysis and design community to call a DFD the parent DFD of the next level DFD, and to call a DFD the child DFD of the preceding level DFD. For example, the context diagram is the parent DFD of the Level-1 DFD, and Level-2 DFDs are the children DFD of the Level-1 DFD. Also, the levels of DFDs are said to become "lower" along with the decomposition.

A key principle of system decomposition is **balancing**. Balancing refers to ensuring that the information presented in the parent DFD is accurately represented in its children DFDs. This does not mean that the information presented in the two generation DFD is identical. Balancing means that the children DFDs can always present more detailed information than the parent DFD does, but must not lose the information presented in the parent DFD.

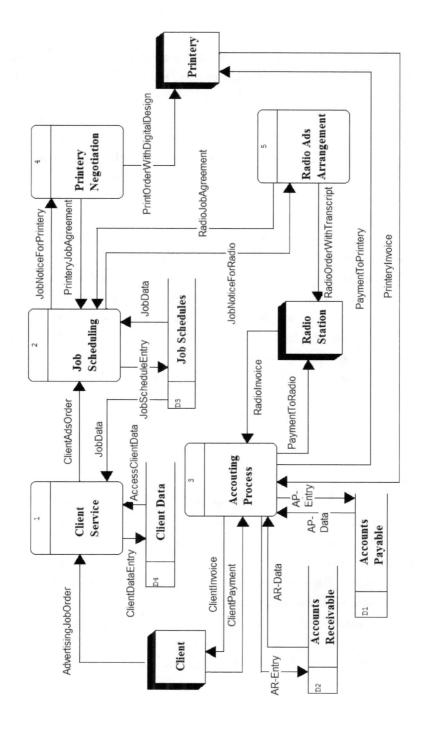

**Figure 4.13. The Level-1 DFD for the Context Diagram in Figure 4.7**

For instance, the context diagram represents the major interactions between the external entities and the system (e.g., job orders, payments, etc.). The secondary interactions between the external entities and the system (e.g., decline notice, payment confirmation, etc.) may not appear in the context diagram in order to make the context diagram succinct. This is consistent with the concept of top-down system decomposition in the day-to-day life. For example, when you zoom-in a map, the highways in the parent map will be kept in the detailed children maps, and the children maps can have secondary routes and paths which are not important to the parent map.

To achieve the balancing between the parent DFD and the children DFDs, simple rules can be applied to the system decomposition.

● Any external entity in the parent DFD must be kept in the children DFDs.

● Any data flow in the parent DFD must be kept in the children DFDs. In some cases, an aggregate data flow in the parent DFD can be split into two or more detailed data flows in the children DFDs, but the data items conveyed by the data flow in the parent DFD must not be lost.

● Any data store in the parent DFD must be kept in the children DFDs. In some cases, a data store in the parent DFD can be split into two or more data stores in the children DFDs, but the data items of the data store in the parent DFD must not be lost.

### 4.5.7. CASE tools

It is the time to learn CASE tools at this point. CASE (Computer Aided Systems Engineering or Computer Aided Software Engineering) tools are a category of software that supports the information systems development process. The support functions of CASE tools vary depending on the tool, ranging from project management to systems diagramming and validation, and even to generating interim prototypes of database and computer code.

The central component of a CASE tool is the **CASE repository** that stores all the diagrams and project information, and is shared by the project team members. The CASE repository ensures the project components consistent. A CASE tool has become a necessary instrument for an information system development project because of the advantages in the following aspects.

- A CASE tool can be used to coordinate the project team activities, and to facilitate knowledge sharing among the project team members.
- A CASE tool allows the project team to follow the standard terminology, the same procedures, the same names of the system components, and the same format of documentation. Thus, the standards of the new system can be created and be enforced through the CASE tool.
- A CASE tool is not just a computer drawing tool. It can have intelligent features to verify the systems analysis and design results to a certain degree, and to ensure balancing between the DFDs. Thus, a CASE tool can reduce errors in the systems development process.
- A CASE tool can generate consistent documents with detailed information for each phase of the SDLC. Thus, a CASE tool can make the systems development process more efficient.

Appendix B provides a detailed tutorial of Visible Analyst, a widely used CASE tool in the industry and education institutions, for the use of DFD.

### 4.5.8. Level-2 diagram

The Level-1 shows the major high-level processes. Each process in the Level-1 DFD can be decomposed into a more detailed DFD, called a Level-2 DFD, in the similar way that the context diagram is decomposed into the Level-1 DFD. The Level-2 DFD may add more detailed secondary data flows and data stores to meet the needs of the detailed processes. The steps of generating a Level-2 DFD are summarized below.

(1) Select a process in the Level-1 DFD to decompose it into the Level-2 DFD.

(2) Include all external entities and data stores which are directly linked to the decomposed process in the Level-1 DFD (see the external entities and data stores marked in bold-line in Figure 4.14) in the Level-2 DFD (see the external entities and data stores marked in bold-line in Figure 4.15).

(3) Include all data flows in the Level-1 DFD which are directly attached to the decomposed process (see the data flows marked in bold-line in Figure 4.14) in the Level-2 DFD (see the data flows marked in bold-line in Figure 4.15).

(4) Replace the decomposed process in the Level-1 DFD with several (e.g., 7 plus or minus 2) detailed processes for the Level-2 DFD, and link all external entities, data flows, and data stores inherited from the Level-1 DFD to the processes in the Level-2 DFD (see the part marked in bold-line in Figure 4.15).

(5) Create data flows between the detailed processes in the Level-2 DFD. New secondary data flows to or from the external entities as well as new detailed data stores may be added if needed (see the data flows to/from Client in fine-line in Figure 4.15). In some cases, an aggregate data flow in the Level-1 DFD can be split into detailed data flows in the Level-2 DFD.

(6) Assign an ID for each detailed process in the Level-2 DFD, following the DFD convention that a process ID in the Level-2 DFD is an extension of the process ID of its parent (Level-1) process. For example, the process ID in the Level-1 DFD is "1", and the its children processes' IDs in the Level-2 DFD would be "1.1", "1.2", and so on (see Figure 4.15).

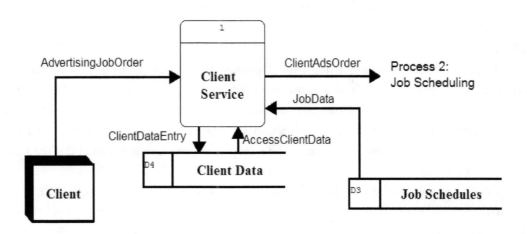

**Figure 4.14. Client Service (Process-1) in Level-1 DFD is to be Decomposed**

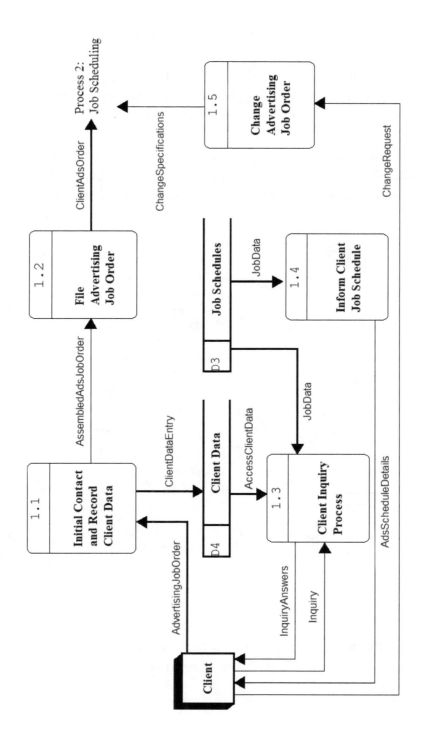

**Figure 4.15. Level-2 DFD of Decomposed Client Service (Process-1)**

In the same way that the process-1 in Figure 4.13 is decomposed into the Level-2 DFD, other four processes in Figure 4.13 can be decomposed into their Level-2 DFDs. In other words, as many as five Level-2 DFDs can be created in this example.

Figure 4.16 illustrates how one system can be decomposed into several levels of DFDs. It also shows the balancing relationships between the levels. Clearly, the top-down system analysis approach is easy to understand if you think about map zooming.

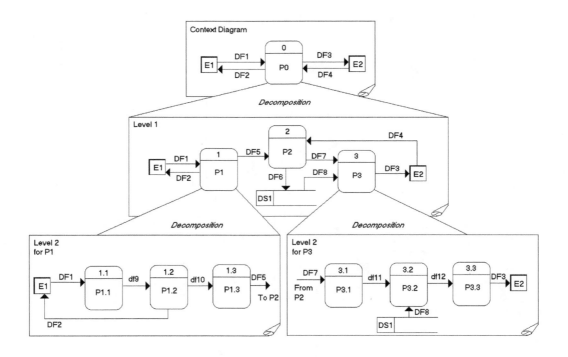

**Figure 4.16. Process Decomposition and Relationships between Levels of Data Flow Diagrams**

### 4.5.9. Scope of system and lower level DFD

As discussed earlier in this section, normally, each step of decomposition of a process in the parent DFD makes 7 plus or minus 2 sub-processes in the child DFD. If the entire system is large, Level-2 DFDs may not be sufficient for describing the processes in great detail. In other words, the number of levels of decomposition depends on the **scope** of the system. For a large information system, the decomposition could reach five or six levels. However, it is rare to have a case with more than seven levels because no single system development project is supposed to practically handle a huge system. In other words, if the system is too large, several systems analysis and design projects are needed.

Conceptually, the principles applied to the decomposition from Level-1 into Level-2 can be applied in the exactly the same way to the decomposition from Level-2 into Level-3, and so on. Then, the question is when the decomposition should end. The commonly used general guideline for decomposition is to reach **primitive processes**, each of which can be described clearly in no more than a dozen lines of short sentences of English, so-called **structured English** (see examples of structured English in Figure 4.20 and Figure 4.26). There is no need to decompose a primitive process because it is simple enough to present its portion of system requirements.

Clearly, the processes in the higher level DFDs are usually aggregate and operate in parallel, and the processes in the lower level DFDs are detailed and can represent sequential steps of workflow.

### 4.5.10. Descriptions of processes, data flows, data stores, and external entities

The decomposition actually articulates the system requirements for the information system by using the DFD tool. At the final stage of system analysis, the system analysts provide detailed descriptions to explain what the processes do and what data are used for the processes. Remember that a non-primitive process is decomposed, and its children DFDs have explained it already. In principle, a non-primitive process does not need narrative descriptions except for an important **decision rule** that specifies several alternative outputs in response to a certain condition(s).

Accordingly, primitive processes, data flows, data stores, and external entities must be described to present precise system requirements.

A CASE tool can provide templates for descriptions of processes, data flows, data stores, and external entities. Suppose the processes in the Level-2 DFD in Figure 4.15 are primitive processes. All elements in the Level-2 DFD need to be described in detail. Examples of descriptions of data flow, data store, external entity, and primitive process are shown in Figure 4.17 through Figure 4.20. Figure 4.20 shows the style of structured English for primitive process descriptions.

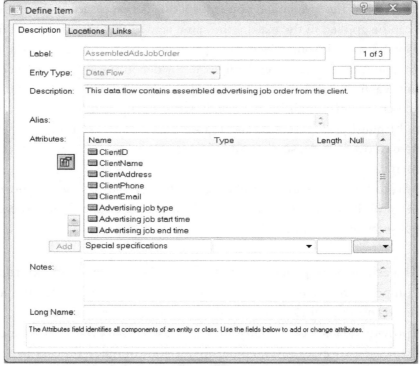

**Figure 4.17. Descriptions of Data Flow**

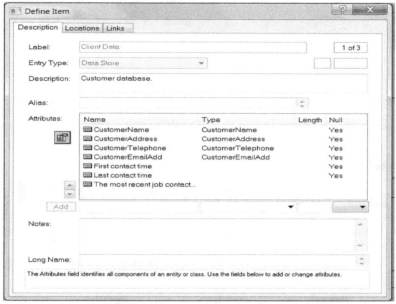

**Figure 4.18. Descriptions of Data Store**

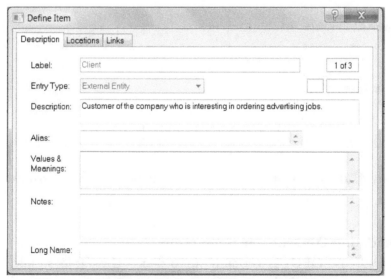

**Figure 4.19. Descriptions of External Entity**

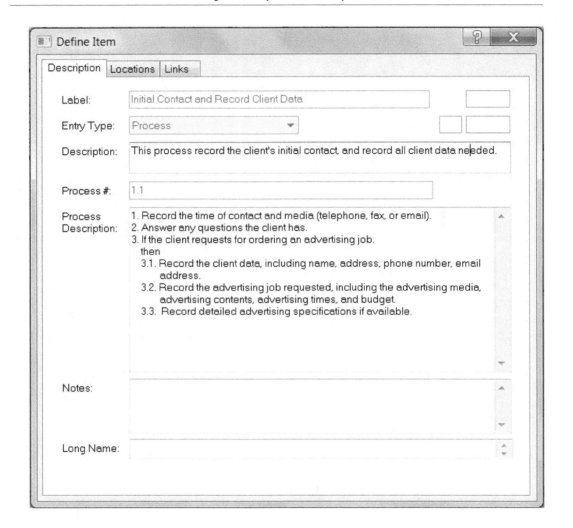

**Figure 4.20. Descriptions of Primitive Process Using Structured English**

### 4.5.11. Validating DFD and common errors

The quality of the DFDs is certainly important. The DFD should be error free. More importantly, the whole set of DFDs for the entire system should be validated.

There are two fundamental types of errors in DFD: syntax errors and semantic errors.

The DFD method is considered to be a "language" that specifies the system requirements. It has its rules as the "grammar" to ensure the accuracy of expression. **Syntax errors** violate these rules and can cause confusion or even significant mistakes.

A set of DFDs with no syntax error may not be correct if this set of DFDs do not represent the true behavior of the real system or the true system requirements. Those errors are not "grammatical" errors, but are the misrepresentation of the meaning of the system, and are called **semantic errors.** The major cause of semantic errors is the system analyst's misunderstanding of the business process or the system requirements. Most CASE tools can detect syntax errors. Also, skilled systems analysts can effectively fix syntax errors. However, semantic errors are much harder to detect, and can cause serious problems for the system development. The best approach to detecting and correcting semantic errors is collaboration and knowledge sharing between the users, the management, and the system analysts.

Beginners of systems analysts need to develop basic skills to detect syntax errors. It is important to check syntax errors in the following three aspects.

### (1) **Syntax errors in the individual DFDs.**

The previous discussion of the DFD method has explained many common syntax errors in individual DFDs. Figure 4.21 summarizes these common syntax errors and explains how one can correct these syntax errors.

Also, the relationships between the data flows and the data stores must be consistent. For instance, if a data flow with the "CustomerName" data item and flows into the "Client Data" data store, then the "Client Data" data store must contain the "CustomerName" data item.

| DFD with Syntax Errors | Explanation | Correct DFD |
|---|---|---|
| 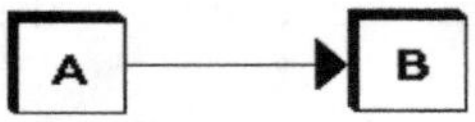 | A direct connection between external entities is not a concern of the system | 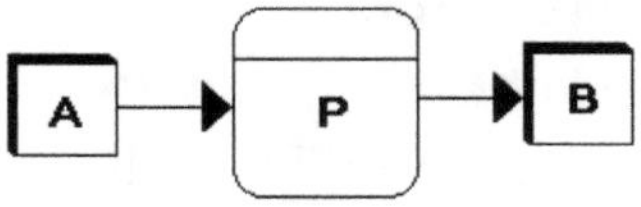 |
| 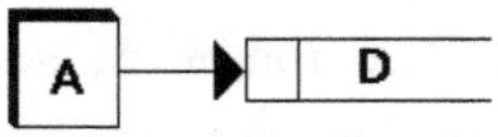 | A connection between an external entity and a data store has to go through a process of the system | 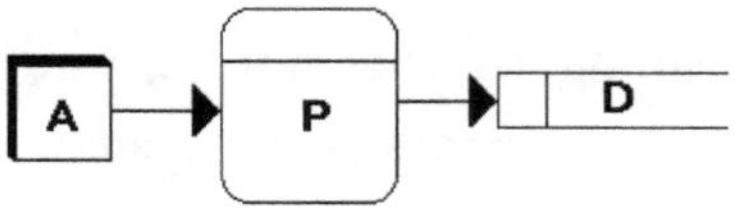 |
| 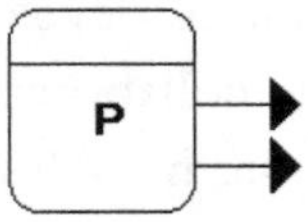 | A process must have at least one input | 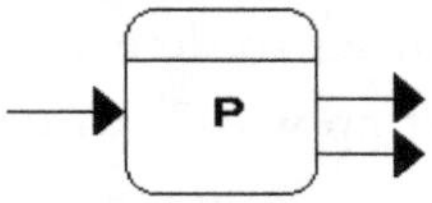 |
| 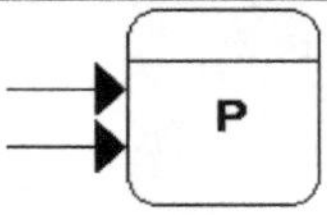 | A process must have at least one output | 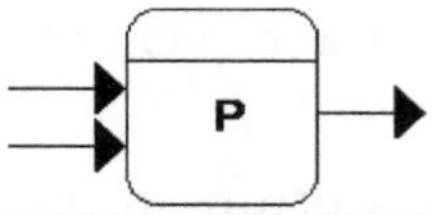 |
| 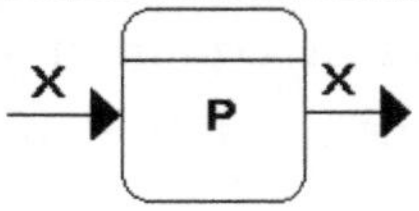 | A process must convert the input into output, and the names of input and output must not be the same | 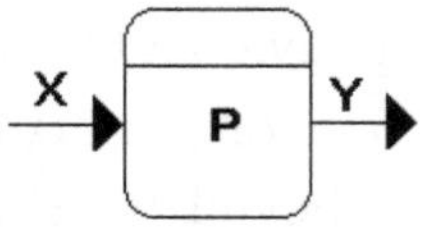 |
| 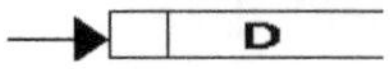 | A data store must be used by a process | 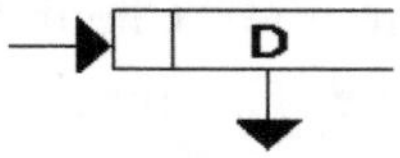 |
| 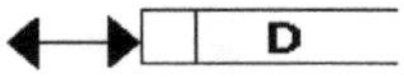 | A two-headed arrow is not allowed, even though the data flow names are the same | 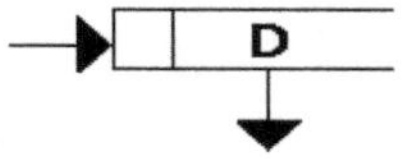 |

**Figure 4.21. Typical Syntax Errors in Individual DFDs**

**(2) Syntax errors in the decomposition.**

One of the common occasions when syntax errors occur is the decomposition. As discussed earlier in the previous sub-sections, there are several rules of balancing between the parent DFD and its children DFDs that ensure the accuracy of the DFDs. A violation of balancing causes syntax errors in the decomposition.

**(3) Syntax errors in the entire analysis project.**

Some syntax errors are not local mistakes, but are mistakes across the entire analysis project. Generally, the entire analysis project must use the standard names of DFD elements across the entire analysis project.

## 4.6. The Use of DFD for Systems Acquisition Development

Before the UML was developed in the late 1990s, DFDs were widely used for system construction based on the structured programming paradigm. In the 1990s, the software engineering field moved towards the object-oriented programming paradigm, and the DFD method is no longer a main-stream method for systems construction, although it could still be used for systems construction (see discussions in Chapter 5). The UML community has attempted to incorporate the DFD methodology as a part of the UML by including the use case modeling method. However, the use case modeling method is basically process descriptions, and does not provide system perspectives. As discussed earlier in this chapter, the UML and BPMN are good tools for systems construction, but are inferior in system acquisition development. In fact, the UML or BPMN describes the system requirements from the viewpoint of systems construction, and the DFD method is more effective than the UML and BPMN in representing the system requirements in the circumstances of systems acquisition development. This section explains this important point.

### 4.6.1. Contrasting the as-is and to-be systems

The DFD method is a powerful tool for contrasting the as-is system and the to-be system visibly and clearly. For example, Figure 4.22a is the context diagram of the as-is system of the advertising agency example. Figure 4.22b is the context diagram of the to-be system of the firm. As you can see, the to-be system includes Manager (see the shaded external entity in the figure) as an additional external entity as well as the additional information services to Manager (see the highlighted data flows). The contrast of the as-is system and the to-be system shows the key difference of the two systems. Clearly, this system development project improves the business process and reaches BPI.

To make a further comparison of the as-is system and the to-be system, the two context diagrams are decomposed into their Level-1 DFDs. Figure 4.23a is the Level-1 DFD of the as-is system, and Figure 4.23b is the Leve-1 DFD of the to-be system. The contrast is further specified in the Level-1 DFDs. In the to-be system Level-1 DFD, the fully shaded process (Process 6 Managerial Reporting) is the newly added process to provide the new information services to the Manager external entity. The partially shaded processes and data stores in the to-be system Level-1 DFD indicate the computerized components that automate the manual as-is system. The new data flows (AP-Data, AR-Data, and AccessClientData) that support the new process (i.e., Process 6) are also added. To reveal its detailed system requirements, the new Process 6 Managerial Reporting is decomposed further into its Level-2 DFD, as shown in Figure 4.24.

To make the contrast of the as-is system and the to-be system easy to observe, the layouts of the DFDs at the corresponding levels should be alike (see Figure 4.22a vs. Figure 4.22b, and Figure 4.23a vs. Figure 4.23b). Technically, the use of copy-paste operations in the CASE tool environment to make the two sets of DFDs not only saves time, but also, more importantly, makes the two sets of DFDs consistent.

For systems acquisition development, the comparison of the as-is system and the to-be system is crucial for the investigation and selection of commercialized software products for the to-be system. In fact, other business process modeling methods are less capable than the DFD method in the aspect of contrasting the as-is system and the to-be system.

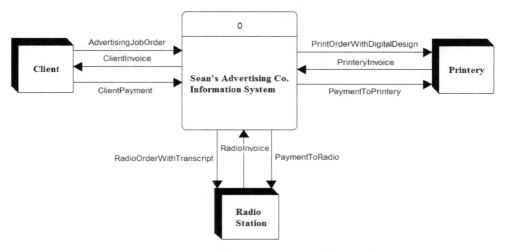

**Figure 4.22a. Context Diagram of the As-Is System**

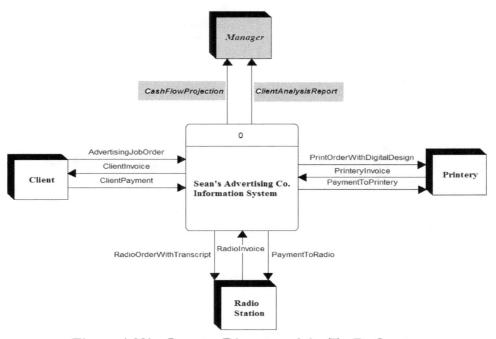

**Figure 4.22b. Context Diagram of the To-Be System**

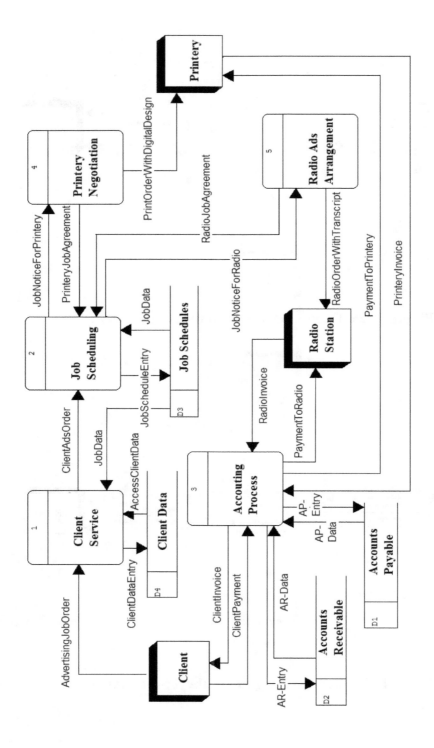

Figure 4.23a. Level-1 DFD of the As-Is system

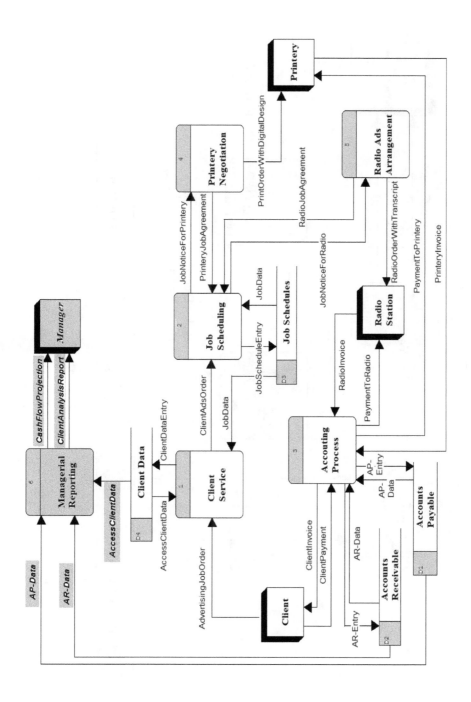

**Figure 4.23b. Level-1 DFD of the To-Be System**

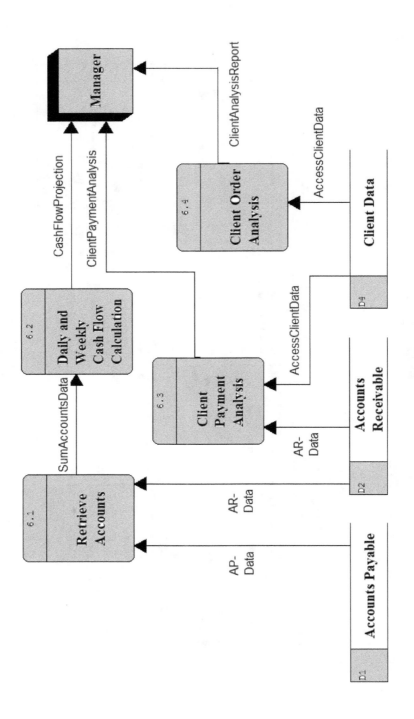

Figure 4.24. Level-2 DFD for the New Process for BPI

### 4.6.2. Specifying functional requirements for system design

As discussed at the beginning of this chapter, the task of the systems analysis phase is to determine the system requirements which include the functional requirements and the nonfunctional requirements. Currently, there is no commonly used formalized method to specify non-functional requirements. In other words, the systems analysts use their subjective judgments to define the nonfunctional requirements in a natural language (e.g., English) for the system design. Like other business process modeling tools, the DFD method is used to specify functional requirements for system design.

#### (1) **Business process**

DFD is an excellent tool for specifying the functional requirements in the business process aspect. Each DFD clearly represents a business process which is a set of business activities performed by human actors and/or the information system to accomplish a specific outcome. A set of DFDs can provide a system perspective of business processes by organizing the processes into a hierarchy.

#### (2) **User-perceived information**

While specifying the functional requirements in the business process aspect, DFDs also specify the functional requirements in the aspect of user-perceived information at the same time. Each process in a DFD associates with its input and output. All requirements of user-perceived inputs and outputs can be represented by a set of DFDs. To provide navigation information for users, instructions on how the user can proceed through the business process can be included in the corresponding process descriptions.

#### (3) **Business rules**

Among the three types of functional requirements (i.e., business processes, information provision, and business rules), business rules are most difficult to formalize in systems analysis due to two major reasons. First, the definitions of business rules are still debatable in the information systems field. Second, the business rules are implemented by the information system through three indepen-dent components: the computing procedures, the database, and the system settings. The three independent components are formalized by many independent modeling methods to specify complicated real-world business rules.

In the context of systems acquisition development DFDs specify two major types of business rules for the functional requirements: workflow and decision rules.

• A **workflow** is a sequence of operations of a routine task which has its start point and end point. As discussed earlier in this chapter, business processes can operate in a parallel pattern or in a sequential order. For representing a workflow using DFD, the fragments that are related to a workflow can be extracted from the DFDs. For example, Figure 4.25 shows a workflow from the Level-1 DFD in Figure 4.23b. This workflow is a fragment of the Level-1 DFD and depicts the sequence of radio advertising job order.

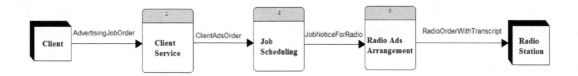

**Figure 4.25. Representing Workflow in DFD**

• A **decision rule** is a statement that specifies the selection of a course of action among several alternative actions in response to a certain condition(s). A general form of decision rules in structured English is

*IF (Condition) THEN (Action).*

In DFD a decision rule is represented in the process descriptions. Figure 4.26 shows an example of decision rules that are extracted from the process description in Figure 4.20.

```
1. Record the time of contact and media (telephone, fax, or email).
2. Answer any questions the client has.
3. If the client requests for ordering an advertising job.
   then
     3.1. Record the client data.
     3.2. Record the advertising job requested.
     3.3. If available, Record detailed advertising specifications.
```

Decision Rules

**Figure 4.26. Decision Rules in Process Descriptions in DFD**

## 4.7. Data Modeling

Business process modeling is the primary systems modeling procedure for systems analysis and design because the business process model of the organization is the central abstraction that describes the business requirements and lays the foundation for other models of the information system. Since business process modeling does not produce the logical structure of data, **data modeling** must be employed in the systems analysis phase to generate a data model for the to-be system. Data modeling is parallel with business process modeling. The two modeling processes in the software system construction are separated. A **data model** is an abstraction that documents the data entities and their relationships commonly using **entity-relationship diagram** (**ERD**) for the database design. The data model developed through the data modeling is independent of the process model because the database should be able to support any potential new business processes. Also, the database of the organization supports the data resource management beyond the business process. As data modeling is normally taught in an independent database course, it is not further discussed in this book. More importantly, in a systems acquisition development project the business process model (i.e., not the data model) is the determinant for the selection of commercialized software product for the to-be system. The chosen software product must have the data model built in by the software producer already. In other words, if the system development applies the systems acquisition strategy, there virtually is no need for data modeling on the project team side.

## 4.8. Systems Analysis Report

A **system analysis report** is a documentation of system requirements for the to-be system. Specifically, it consists of the following important items.

• The complete definition of the project scope.

• The problems of the as-is system, and the objective of the to-be system.

• The system requirements, including all information collected by the requirements determination process.

• The business process models of the as-is system and the to-be system. If the system development project is a systems construction project, the data model for the to-be system is also included.

• A proposal for the systems design phase.

The systems analysis report must go through an approval process in accordance with the structure and rules of the organization. Once it is approved, the system development cycle moves to the systems design phase.


## *Key Terms*

Systems analysis phase
System requirement
Functional requirement
    Business process
    User-perceived information
    Business rules
Nonfunctional requirement
Usability
Scalability

Requirement information collection
    methods
Experiencing and observation
Interview
Questionnaire
Joint analytical development (JAD)
System modeling
Business process modeling
Business process
Operational process

Management process

Supporting process

Business process model

Business process modeling tools

Data flow diagram (DFD)

  Top-down approach

  Decomposition

The Unified Modeling Language
    (UML)

Business Process Modeling Notation
    (BPMN)

Elements of DFD

  External entity

  Process

  Data flow

  Data store

Context diagram

Decomposition

Segment

Heuristics

Balancing

Level-1 DFD

Level-2 DFD

CASE tool

CASE repository

Syntax error

Semantic error

Common syntax errors of DFD

Business rules

Workflow

Decision rule

System requirements represented by
    DFDs

System analysis reports

## *Exercises of Systems Analysis and Design Course Project*

1. Draw the context DFD for the as-is system, and the context DFD for the to-be system.

2. Decompose the context diagrams into a Level 1 DFD. Keep balancing and eliminate syntax errors. Each group member contributes her/his segments.

3. Each group member examines at least one process in the Level 1 DFD and decomposes it into a Level 2 DFD.

4. Highlight the differences between the as-is system and the to-be system in the aspects of BPA and BPI.

5. Describe the primitive processes.

6. Summarize the systems analysis results.

# CHAPTER 5. SYSTEMS DESIGN

The **systems design phase** determines how the to-be system is created and how it will operate in terms of hardware, software, networking, system personnel, and operational procedures. The objective of the systems design phase is to create a set of system specifications for the to-be system. A **system specification** is a structured collection of information that describes all technological components needed for the to-be system to accomplish the system requirements modeled in the systems analysis report. A successful systems design process generates complete system specifications that can lead to a smooth system implementation.

Obviously, the tasks of systems design for systems construction development are quite different from that for systems acquisition development, because a systems construction involves the designs of many components of application software for the to-be system. Nevertheless, the systems design phase has three interactive design tasks.

(1) Designing the system infrastructure for the to-be system.

(2) Designing the alternatives of commercialized software products for the to-be system in systems acquisition development; or, designing the application software specifications for the to-be system in systems construction development.

(3) Designing the system architecture, and selecting hardware and networking of the to-be system.

## 5.1. Systems Design for Systems Acquisition Development

**Systems design for systems acquisition** development is the process of defining the specifications of system infrastructure, system architecture, alternatives software products for the to-be system to satisfy the determined system requirements.

### 5.1.1. System infrastructure design

**System infrastructure** refers to the basic physical structures and the organizational information technology (IT) competence needed for the operation of an information system.

(1) **Basic physical structures** of system infrastructure include the following major attributes.

- Technical facilities of the information system, such as computers, networks, and other equipment;
- Computing tools, such as computer languages, database management systems, and office automation tools;
- Equipment storage, such as computing center;
- Power system;
- Telecommunication, such as wired, wireless (wifi, WiMAX).

(2) **Organizational IT competence** of system infrastructure includes the following major attributes.

- The existing and potential users' computer literacy;
- The existing and potential users' information literacy;
- Procedures, policy, and rules relevant to the current information system;
- Computing support facilities of the current information system, such as IT department.

The **system infrastructure design** of the systems design phase determines the specifications of the system infrastructure for the to-be system. It is rather artistic, and needs great managerial skills to address the above attributes of system infrastructure for the organization.

### 5.1.2. Design of alternatives of application software products

In its broad sense, **design** refers to making a plan of actions. This concept is particularly applicable to the systems acquisition case, because making a plan to choose an ideal application software product on the software market for the to-be system is the design task at this stage of systems acquisition development.

Since nowadays there is no commonly applied format of business application software specifications that can be used for describing the features of application software products for consumers, producers and vendors of commercialized business application software products use free-format descriptions and *ad hoc* style demos to market their products. Consumers have few guidelines for examination of the business processes that are embedded in the application software products. The systems development professionals have to use their own knowledge and judgments to compare the features of application software products against the system requirements for the to-be system. This reality brings up many challenges for systems acquisition development. Generally, the following steps are necessary in making a plan for systems acquisition.

(1) **Exploring** the software market to obtain a long list of candidate application software products.

The system analysts must apply their system thinking skills and general systems analysis knowledge to widely search the application software market to collect information about the candidate application software products for the to-be system.

For a large information system, ERP systems are ideal. There are a few popular large ERP systems such as SAP, Oracle Applications, and The Sage Group. There are also small scale ERP systems such as Microsoft Dynamics. It is necessary for the system analysts to consult with the local vendor of an ERP system to receive detailed information on the software product.

Recently, open source ERP systems are widely available for business, such as webERP, Compiere, PostBooks, Opentaps, and OpenBravo. An open source software product is free to use, but has little direct system support and services.

For medium and small scale systems, packaged off-the-shelf application software products are ideal. Search engines (such as *<www.Google.com>* and *<www.Bing.com>*) are useful for exploring the application software products on the market. Using the keywords of the business application concerned (such as "*advertising agent management information system software*"), one can find plentiful application software products. Usually, if the software product is well marketed, the software package producer must provide an inviting, informative, and comprehensive demo of the product. To receive a detailed demo, you may have to provide your email address and the purpose of reviewing the demo in order for the producer to keep records, but must not provide your personal identity (such as social security number) or financial information (such as credit card number). The system analysts may also consult with IT consultants and software vendors to explore packaged software products that can be considered for the to-be system.

For generic business applications, such as online shops, where data security and response time are not major concerns, SaaS can be an option for systems acquisition development.

(2) **Confining** the candidate products to generate a short list of alternatives.

After exploring the software market, the systems analysts confine the candidate products and generate a short list with a limited number of **alternatives** (e.g., three alternatives) that are worth further examination in great detail for the to-be system.

(3) **Examining** the alternatives in great detail against the system requirements.

Examining the alternatives is a labor intensive job for the system analysts. As pointed out earlier in this sub-section, for the time being, there is no structured method for evaluating a commercialized software product. The system analysts rely on their subjective knowledge and judgment to assess whether and how the software product meets the system requirements determined through the system analysis phase. The system analysts need to investigate each of the alternative software products in the following aspects before a conclusion can be possibly obtained.

- Demo of the supported business processes;
- Documentation, including reference documents, operation manuals, and tutorials;
- Overall performance records, and tests documentation;
- Comments and reviews from its consumers.

(4) **Making a recommendation** for the selection of application software product for the to-be system.

At the end of the design stage, the system analysts apply their decision making skills and participate in an intensive decision process to recommend one application software product among the alternatives at the end of the systems design phase.

Figure 5.1 illustrates the roles of system analysts in selecting application software product.

**Decision matrix** is a simple instrument for making a recommendation for the selection of application software product for the to-be system. A decision matrix is a table of decision factors and values that allows the system design team to systematically identify, analyze, and rate the relationships between the factors.

In the present case of selection of application software products, a decision matrix lists $M$ **alternatives** (e.g., $M=3$ alternative software products) and $N$ **decision criteria** (e.g., $N=25$ primitive processes for functional requirements). Each cell of the $M \times N$ matrix represents a **decision factor**, as shown in the example of Figure 5.2.

A commonly used method for decision matrix is the **weighted average method**. This method assigns a relative importance weight to each decision criterion. The system design team then rates the performance of each alternative software product with respect to each decision criterion and obtains the values of the decision factors. The rating value of each decision factor is multiplied by the corresponding criterion importance weight to calculate a weighted score. These weighted scores of each alternative are then summed over all the criteria to obtain one aggregate weighted score for each alternative software product. The software product with the highest aggregate weighted score is considered to have the best overall performance. This weighted average method is simple, but has its limitation in that the weights and the values of decision factors are subjective.

Figure 5.2 is an example of decision matrix for the functional requirements of the Sean's Advertising Co. Information System which is modeled in Figure 4.23b. Figure 5.3 is an example of decision matrix for nonfunctional requirements. Appendix C exhibits more detailed examples of decision matrix.

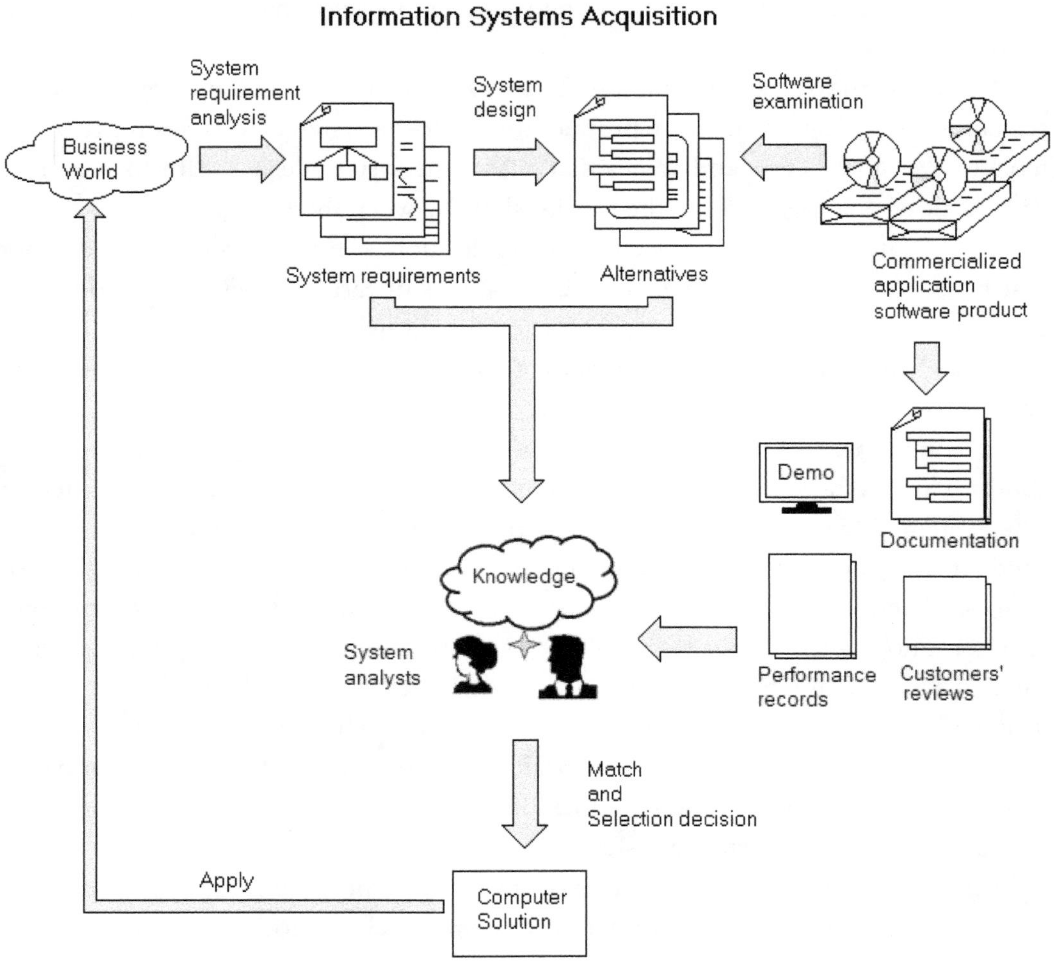

**Information Systems Acquisition**

**Figure 5.1. Roles of System Analysts in Application Software Selection**

| Functionality | Weight | Alternative1 | Alternative 2 | Alternative 3 |
|---|---|---|---|---|
| P1.  Client Service | - | - | - | - |
|    P1.1. Initial Contact and Record Client Data | | | | |
|    P1.2. File Advertising Job Order | | | | |
|    P1.3. Client Inquiry Process | | | | |
|    P1.4. Inform Client Job Schedule | | | | |
|    P1.5. Change Advertising Job Order | | | | |
| P2.  Job Scheduling | - | - | - | - |
|    P2.1. . . . . . | | | | |
|    P2.2. . . . . . | | | | |
| . . . . . . | | | | |
| P3.  Accounting Process | - | - | - | - |
|    P3.1. . . . . . | | | | |
|    P3.2. . . . . . | | | | |
| . . . . . . | | | | |
| P4. Printery Negotiation | - | - | - | - |
|    P4.1. . . . . . | | | | |
|    P4.2. . . . . . | | | | |
| . . . . . . | | | | |
| P5. Radio Ads Arrangement | - | - | - | - |
|    P5.1. . . . . . | | | | |
|    P5.2. . . . . . | | | | |
| . . . . . . | | | | |
| P6. | - | - | - | - |
|    P6.1. . . . . . | | | | |
|    P6.2. . . . . . | | | | |
| . . . . . . | | | | |
| **Total Scores** | - | | | |

**Figure 5.2. Example of Decision Matrix for Functional Requirements for Selecting Application Software Product**

| Non-Functional Requirements | Weight | Alternative1 | Alternative 2 | Alternative 3 |
|---|---|---|---|---|
| 1. Usability | - | - | - | - |
| 1.1. Easy to use - Quality of the user interface design | | | | |
| 1.2. Error tolerance | | | | |
| 1.3. Documentation (reference documents, manuals, and tutorials) | | | | |
| 2. Security | | | | |
| 3. Vendor | - | - | - | - |
| 3.1. Reputation | | | | |
| 3.2. Services | | | | |
| 3.3. Business alliance | | | | |
| 3.4. Training availability | | | | |
| 3.5. Standardization | | | | |
| 4. Performance | - | - | - | - |
| 4.1. Reliability | | | | |
| 4.2. Scalability | | | | |
| 4.3. Speed | | | | |
| 5. Others | | | | |
| 5.1. Multiple language | | | | |
| 5.2. Leasing / licensing options | | | | |
| **Total Scores** | - | | | |

**Figure 5.3. Example of Decision Matrix for Nonfunctional Requirements for Selecting Application Software Product**

### 5.1.3. Comprehensive decision making for system acquisition

Since the selection of commercial software product is crucial for the to-be system, in many cases the project team's design of alternative software products and its recommendation may not be the final decision for the organization. At the end of the systems design phase for systems acquisition development, the system development project team might want to involve the top management, the representatives of key stakeholders, and the potential users for making the final decision on the selection of commercialized software product for the to-be system.

Software product selection is a typical **multiple criteria decision making** problem. There have been many sophisticated models of multiple criteria decision making models. Each model has its advantages and limitations. More importantly, the concept of multiple criteria decision making is evolving into a broader notion of decision process serving as knowledge sharing and collaboration in the organization.

The system requirements for systems acquisition can be organized into a complete criteria hierarchy, as illustrated in Figure 5.4, which provides a device for group decision making. **Analytical hierarchy process (AHP)** is the most feasible, established, and widely applied method of group decision making in this case. AHP is a multi-attribute decision-making technique through prioritizing the alternatives. It is actually an extension of the simple weighted average decision matrix method. There have been many AHP software packages on the market. The decision making process for system acquisition using the AHP technique includes the following steps.

Step 1: Construct a hierarchy of system requirements for the system acquisition (Figure 5.4).

Step 2: Starting from the top of the hierarch, for each sub-tree of the hierarchy, conduct the pairwise comparison by the decision team to reveal the comparative importance between the two requirements.

Step 3: Using the principal eigenvector of the pairwise comparison matrix manipulated by scaling ratio, find the comparative weight among the requirements for the sub-tree.

Step 4: Repeat the comparisons from top of the hierarchy until all relative weights have been determined.

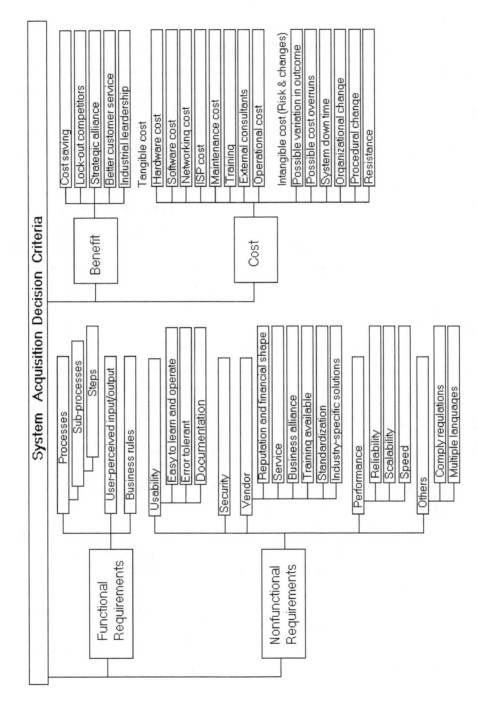

**Figure 5.4. General Criteria Hierarchy for Decision Marking for Systems Acquisition**

Step 5: For each of the system alternatives, assign the values to each of the hierarchical system requirements (Figure 5.4). The values could be objective data, or subjective estimations.

Step 6: Based on the relative weights of the system requirements and the values of the system requirements for each systems alternative, calculate the score of each system alternative. The system with the highest score will be the best decision for system acquisition.

Clearly, any single model, including the AHP model, is imperfect in the unstructured decision making context. The most important point here is that the organization can make informed decision on the selection of commercialized software product for the to-be system through collaboration among all key players in the organization.

## 5.1.4. Backward-design

The selected commercial application software product may not have an exact match of its functionalities to the system requirements of the to-be system as defined by the systems analysis phase. System **backward-design** in the system design phase of systems acquisition development is the process to fully investigate the difference between what are needed as specified in the system requirements and what are available in the selected application software product, and to design an approach to coping with the difference in the system implementation.

If the application software product provides surplus functions and features, there is an opportunity for the organization to fully utilize the functions and features for the BPI. The system backward-design can explore new BPI components for the to-be system, including

- new operational processes that make the organizational operations more complete;
- new supporting processes that make the organizational operations more perfective;
- new managerial processes that make the organizational decisions more effective; and
- new information resources that make the system more informative.

It is also possible that the selected software product is short of required functions and features. If this is the case, a gap between the analyzed system requirements and the future to-be system occurs. In the present context of systems acquisition development, a **gap** refers to the shortfall disparity between the functionalities and features of the recommended commercial software product and the system requirements determined by the system analysis.

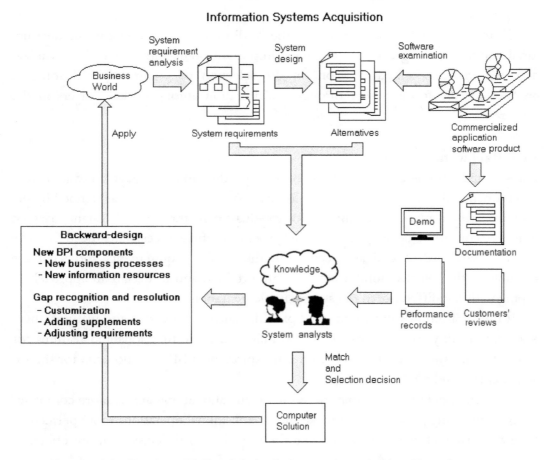

**Figure 5.5. Backward-Design in Systems Acquisition Development**

Normally, the gap should not be significant; otherwise the software product should not be adopted. A typical small business information system project may not find any gap. Nevertheless, the systems design team must not overlook the gap issue.

**Gap recognition and resolution** is the process that the system design team identifies the gap and makes a plan to close the gap. Generally, there are three types of remedies to close a gap: customizing the software product, adding supplemental software products, and adjusting the system requirements.

## (1) **Customizing the software product**

**Customizing** actually transforms the product software in tailor-made software, because the software product in its standardized form causes a gap for the to-be system. Customizing can result in a situation where the system requirements are not adjusted, which puts less pressure on the project team as well as the users. This may positively add to the recommended application software product for the to-be system. However, customizing is a complicated issue and needs to acquire consultancy from the software producer. In most cases of small and medium-sized business, customizing is not an option.

## (2) **Adding supplemental software product**

Adding a supplemental software product can bridge a gap. For example, a seafood company is developing an information system for its seafood business, has examined a dozen commercial software products for seafood business operations, and finally finds a good software product which is suitable for the to-be system. The recommended software product can perform all operational functions ranging from grading, inventory management, shipping, sales management, scheduling, etc., but is short of marketing campaign functions. The design team considers that a supplemental software product for marketing campaign can be easily integrated into the to-be system to fulfill the system requirements.

Adding a supplemental software product will certainly increase the cost of the to-be system. More importantly, the data compatibility and the interfaces between the central application software and the supplemental software could be complicated. In the above example, the coupling relationship between the seafood operation management software and the marketing campaign software is insubstantial, and the data compatibility and the interface between the two parts are not a serious concern to the system design team. Thus, adding supplemental software product can be a solution of closing the gap in this case.

### (3) Adjusting system requirements

If it is difficult to find a supplemental software product, or there is no other way to trade-off the costs and benefit, adjusting system requirements to close the gap might be necessary. **Adjusting system requirements** is to redefine or sacrifice the system requirements that are not supported by the selected software product. Adjusting system requirements is more sensible for causing potential resistance in the usage of the recommended software product, because it might alter the tasks and responsibilities of the users of the to-be system. However, while the product software is not altered, better support and service levels are possible.

### 5.1.5. System architecture design

**System architecture** refers to the structure of a computational resources network. It specifies the topology of computational recourses including
- hardware (PCs, servers, routers, switches, and printers and other peripheral equipment);
- computer networks (LANs);
- operating systems;
- databases; and
- application software across the computer network.

The **system architecture design** plans the system architecture for the to-be system by providing detailed specifications for each of the computational resource components of the network.

A system architecture design starts with a computer network design. As explained earlier in this book, normally a data communication course and its textbooks fully cover the knowledge body about computer networking. Nevertheless, basic knowledge of computer networking would be sufficient for a systems acquisition development project. This paragraph provides a brief overview of computer networking for system architecture design. Physically, a typical wired network has a number of computers linked together by special cabling through devices called **switches**. Switches connect to another kind of device called a **router**, and routers in turn connect to yet another device known as a broadband **gateway**. A gateway is a communication device that acts as an entrance to another network. In the network for an enterprise, a computer server acting as a gateway node is also acting as a proxy server and a firewall server. Homes and small business firms get Internet access from either a local cable company or a phone company which provides the Internet access and is called an **Internet Service Provider** (**ISP**). In order for a home or a small business to gain access to the Internet, an ISP provides a special type of gateway which is also commonly referred to as a cable modem or **DSL modem**. A router is to connect one network (e.g., the Internet) to another (e.g., local area network). A large organization often uses multiple routers to link the different local area networks of departments (e.g., Production plan, Marketing, and Human Resources). In the context of a typical small business network, the router is the intermediary between the local area network and the ISP. Routers designed for small business networks usually have a firewall built into them. Computers are linked to a router and to each other through switches. In a wired network, the actual physical connections are made with cables. Routers designed for home and small business networks (with less than 8 computers) typically have the switching technology built into it; that is, one device performs both functions.

Currently, there is no standard diagramming tool or standard documentation form for system architecture design despite of the advance of information technology. On the other hand, for information technology professionals, it does not matter what tools are used for system architecture design as long as the tools communicate the system architecture specifications. It has become a norm that systems designers just use whatever tools the organization has already adopted or they agree upon. Figure 5.6 shows an example of diagram of system network design.

Figure 5.7 shows an example of computer equipment layout plan of a business office.

Next, for each of the components of the computer network, the system designer provides technical specifications. As computer hardware products and computer networking devices follow common specification standards, the system designer's job is to ensure the chosen components of the network are compatible, and to document the technical specifications along with references. Figure 5.8 shows a hypothetical example of specifications of a server.

Nowadays, cloud computing has become a topical issue in the information technology industry. In an ideal cloud computing environment, it is no longer for ordinary business organizations to own and manage their system architecture. Cloud computing provides computational power, software, data access, and storages as services through the Internet without requirement for the end-user knowledge of the physical location and configuration of the systems of the services providers. Although the perceived advantages of the cloud computing model are extraordinary, cloud computing technology is still in its very early stage. Generally, a global system architecture must be developed to allow business organizations to utilize all available services on the Internet without their own system architecture. For the time being, such a global system architecture is yet to come.

## 5.2. Systems Design for Systems Construction Development

**Systems design for systems construction** development is the process of defining the specifications for the system infrastructure, the system architecture and its components, the database, the user interface, and the program modules for constructing the to-be system to satisfy the determined system requirements.

System infrastructure design for systems construction is not much different from system infrastructure design for systems acquisition development, because system infrastructure concerns basic physical structures and organizational IT competence.

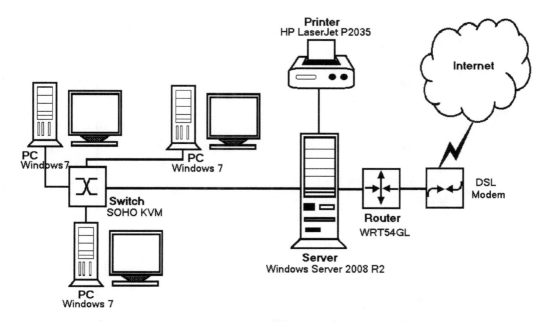

**Figure 5.6. Network Diagram**

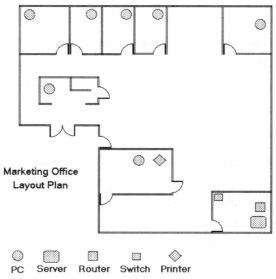

**Figure 5.7.  Computing Equipment Layout Plan**

```
┌─────────────────────────────────────────────────────────────┐
│                                                             │
│  ServerExample X1                                           │
│                                                             │
│  An Intel-based, 2-socket/1U server                         │
│                                                             │
│  Specifications                                             │
│                                                             │
│  Processor                                                  │
│  Intel® Xeon® E5620 2.4Ghz, 12M Cache, Turbo, HT, 1066MHz Max Mem │
│                                                             │
│  Operating System                                           │
│  Windows Server 2008 R2                                     │
│                                                             │
│  Chassis                                                    │
│  Chassis for Up to Six 2.5-Inch Hard Drives                 │
│                                                             │
│  Memory                                                     │
│  4GB Memory (4x1GB), 1333MHz Single Ranked UDIMMs for 1 Processor, Advanced ECC │
│                                                             │
│  Hard Drive                                                 │
│  250GB 7.2K RPM SATA 2.5" Hot Plug Hard Drive               │
│                                                             │
│  Optical Drive                                              │
│  DVD ROM SATA, Internal                                     │
│                                                             │
│  Warranty                                                   │
│  3Yr Basic Hardware WarrantyRepair: 5x10 HW-Only, 5x10 NBD Onsite │
│                                                             │
└─────────────────────────────────────────────────────────────┘
```

**Figure 5.8. Hypothetical Example of Specifications of Server**

When designing the system architecture for systems construction development, the system development team can have more flexibility in choosing hardware and networking because compatibility constraints can be relaxed through the application software construction. As hardware and data communication networking are more or less standardized these days and are not the objects of systems construction, system architecture design for systems construction development is also not significantly different from system architecture design for systems acquisition development.

As the major object of construction is business application software, the design of application software in systems construction development is extensive. This textbook describes the general concepts of systems design for systems construction development succinctly.

### 5.2.1. Design of physical business process model

In the systems analysis phase, the system requirements are described in a business process model, which is called a **logical business process model** because it illustrates the essential requirements for the system but does not specify how these essential requirements can be accomplished. For systems acquisition development, the systems design team uses a logical business process model as the criteria for evaluating commercial software products, and is not concerned about how these commercial software products actually implement the logical business process models. However, in systems construction development, the systems design team has to create a **physical business process model** to specify systems construction details and to document how the logical business process model can be implemented using software construction techniques. The physical business process model for the to-be system not only shows what the to-be system is or does, but also shows how the to-be system is technically implemented. Therefore, physical business process models are construction-dependent because they reflect technological choices of the designers.

In general, a physical business processing model contains the same components as the logical business process model, and also includes additional technical details for construction such as

- user-system boundary;
- computer programming languages used for the computerized processes;
- data communication and data transmission media; and
- database management systems for the computerized data stores.

Figure 5.9 is an example of physical DFD for physical business process modeling. This physical DFD is created based on the logical DFD in Figure 4.2 which represents a client service process. Figure 5.9 shows the system boundary, computer languages and tools (PHP, MS Word, HTML), database management system (MySQL), and data communication and data transmission media (email, ASCII). It also indicates the computerized components of the system by shaded processes and the shaded data stores.

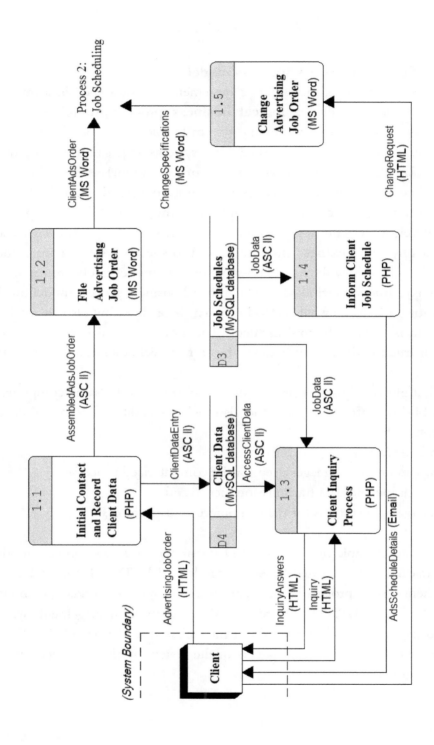

Figure 5.9. Physical DFD for Physical Business Process Modeling

### 5.2.2. Database design

**Database design** is to determine how data are stored and accessed. Database design includes database logical design and database physical design based on the data models obtained in the systems analysis phase. The deliverables of database design include database logical design specifications and database physical design specifications. Detailed database design techniques are normally taught in an independent database course and its companion textbooks.

### 5.2.3. User interface design

A **user interface** is the component of the information system by which users interact with the system. The goal of user interface design is to achieve a high **usability** of the system. The user interface of the system allows the users to access the system through

- **input** - to enter data for operating the system;
- **output** - to receive information from the system; and
- **navigation** - to find a direction of action.

Design of user interface is neither less important nor easier than design of core functionalities of applications. Currently, **graphical user interface (GUI)** is the most common type of user interface. GUI allows users to interact with the system with images rather than text commands. A GUI represents the information and actions available to the user through graphical icons, menus, buttons, and visual indicators. The design of user interface includes two tasks: user interface structure design and user interface view design.

(1) The **user interface structure design** defines the structure of the user interface that allows the users to fully access the functionalities of the system. **User interface structure diagram** can be used as a tool for user interface structure design, as illustrated in Figure 5.10. Clearly, a user interface structure diagram can be viewed as a flat hierarchy of the corresponding functionalities modeled in the set of DFDs for the system. This is another example that demonstrates why DFDs provide a base for the systems design.

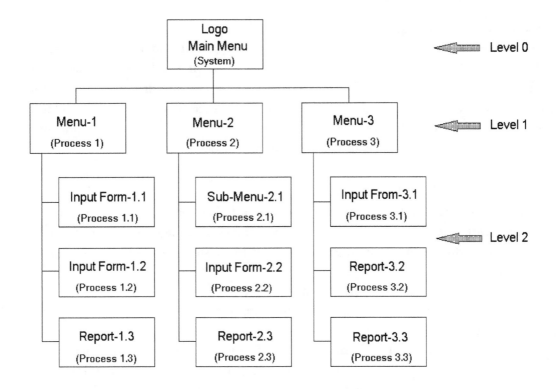

**Figure 5.10. User Interface Structure Diagram**

(2) The **user interface view design** defines the GUI screens and the report layouts of the system. A user interface view design is rather artistic, and involves such disciplines as ergonomics and psychology. **Principles of user interface view design** are intended to produce a user interface which makes it easy, efficient, and enjoyable to operate the system for the users to produce the desired results. There are several general principles for user interface design, as described below.

● Simplicity - A user interface should be simple and easy to use while communicating clearly in the user's own language.

- Visibility - A user interface should make all needed options and materials for a given task visible without confusion.
- Informing - A user interface should keep the user informed of actions or interpretations without information overloading.
- Tolerance - A user interface should make the system flexible and tolerant of operational errors (e.g., un-do operations).
- Consistency - A user interface should maintain consistency with purpose across the entire system.
- Inviting - A use interface should be attractive.

As pointed out earlier in this book, nowadays the majority of business organizations develop their information systems through systems acquisition of commercialized software products which have the user interfaces built in already. Nevertheless, the above general principles of user interface view design are also applicable to the assessment of user interfaces in systems acquisition development.

### 5.2.4. Programs design

Computerized business processes are executed by application computer programs (or application software). Application software designers design the application computer programs based on the systems analysis results of systems requirements. The application computer programs are designed to accomplish the automated business processes. The techniques used for application software design falls into two types of computer programming: structured programming design (e.g., for C and traditional COBOL languages) and object-oriented programming design (e.g., for VB.NET and Java languages). The deliverables of the programs design include diagrams of structured programs design, object-oriented programs design, and other programs specifications. Detailed programs design techniques are normally taught in independent programming courses and their companion textbooks.

## 5.3. Systems Design Report

A **system design report** is a documentation of system specifications for the to-be system. As discussed in this chapter, the form of application software specifications for systems construction development is highly different from that for systems acquisition development. Nevertheless, the following important items should be included in a system design report.

- The system infrastructure design of the to-be system.
- The application software specifications of the to-be system.

    For systems acquisition, application software specifications include:
    - the alternatives of software products for the to-be system;
    - demos and trial records investigated for each alternative software product;
    - supporting documents reviewed for each alternative software product;
    - the decision matrices for functional requirements and nonfunctional requirements for the recommendation;
    - the backward-design for the recommended application software product; and
    - the organization-wide comprehensive decision on the selection of the application software product for the to-be system.

    For systems construction, application software specifications include:
    - the physical business process models for the to-be system;
    - the database design for the to-be system;
    - the user interface design for the to-be system;
    - the programs design for the to-be system; and
    - the recommended computational instruments (i.e., the database management systems, the computer programming languages, and other software tools.) for construction.

- The system architecture specifications, including hardware, networking, and operating systems, for the to-be system.
- A proposal for the systems implementation phase.

The systems design report must go through an approval process in accordance with the structure and rules of the organization. Once it is approved, the system development cycle moves to the systems implementation phase.

### *Key Terms*

Systems design phase
System infrastructure
System infrastructure design
System specification
Systems design for systems acquisition
Business application software
   specification
Systems acquisition planning
  Exploring
  Confining
  Examining
Alternative software product
   investigation
  Demo
  Documentation
  Customers' review
  Performance reports
Decision matrix
Decision criteria
Alternatives
Weighted average method

Analytical hierarchy process (AHP)
Backward-design
Gap
Gap recognition and resolution
Customization
Adding supplemental software
   product
Adjusting system requirements
System architecture
System architecture design
Logical business process model
Physical business process model
User interface design
Usability
Graphical user interface (GUI)
User interface structure diagram
User interface view design
Principles of user interface design
Programs design
System design reports

## *Exercises of Systems Analysis and Design Course Project*

1. Search application software products alternatives for the to-be system.

2. Select three most impressive application software products alternatives.

3. Examine the three alternatives and develop decision matrices for functional requirements and nonfunctional requirements.

4. Select one of the alternatives.

5. Search hardware which compatible with the selected software product for the to-be system.

6. Search networking equipment for the to-be system.

7. Summarize the system design results.

# CHAPTER 6. SYSTEMS IMPLEMENTATION

The **systems implementation phase** builds the to-be system based on the system specifications provided by the design phase, and converts the as-is system to the to-be system. It includes the following major steps.

(1) Generating the to-be system. As discussed in Chapter 2, the actual way of generating the to-be system depends on the systems development strategy. For systems acquisition development, installation of the software product, configuring or making customization if needed, and data conversion are the major tasks of this step. For systems construction development, the actual construction for the to-be system through the use of computer tools takes place in this step.

(2) Converting the as-is system to the to-be system, and testing the to-be system.

(3) Establishing system support facilities for the new information system.

(4) Documenting the system implementation.

## 6.1. System Implementation for Systems Acquisition Development

The system implementation activities for systems acquisition development in this phase include system installation, customization of the software product, data conversion, and system tests.

### 6.1.1. System installation

System installation in these days has become more and more simple. Hardware (servers and client PCs) installation usually needs only a few steps of configuration. Network installation depends upon many factors, such as the Internet provider in the location, wiring or wireless network setting, and the topology of the local network of the organization. The commercial software product for the system should be easy to install if the quality of the product is good. If the software product is used in the client-server architecture environment, it usually includes two parts: one part is installed on the server of the system, and the other part is installed on the client PCs.

### 6.1.2. Configuring ERP system, or customizing software product

An ERP system typically builds-in many changeable parameters that modify the ways of system operations. For example, an organization can select FIFO or LIFO for the principle of cost accounting operations. **Configuring** an ERP system is to set these parameters to meet the organization's specific situations. A large ERP system must be configured before it can operate.

Some commercialized software products allow **customizing** to transform the product software in a tailor-made way to provide a particular feature(s). Customizing can be expensive and complicated, and can delay the implementation.

### 6.1.3. Data conversion

**Data conversion** is the process of moving and restructuring the data from the current system to the new system. For example, a manual system has data on papers, and some data are incomplete. It is a considerable job to digitalize these data so that the new computerized system can store them. Digital data can have various data formats depending on the system. If the to-be system and the as-is system use different digital data formats, a data conversion software tool must be applied for the data conversion. Data conversion is critical to the implementation success and requires significant preparation. The following steps can structure data conversion process.

- Identify the data for conversion.
- Determine data conversion timing.
- Decide the new data formats.
- Select data conversion methods and tools.
- Define data archiving policies and procedures.

### 6.1.4. System tests for acquired system

**System tests for the acquired system** cover many types of tests of the software product acquired for the system, as explained below.

- Functional requirement tests - whether the system functional requirements are met.
- Reliability tests - whether the system is reliable.

128

- Usability tests - whether the system is easy to use.
- Performance tests - whether the system can handle the workload properly.
- Error handling tests - whether the system is tolerant to operational mistakes.
- Security tests - whether the system is secured from unauthorized access and disasters.
- Scalability tests - whether the system can handle the foreseeable growth of workload.

Clearly, the system tests for the acquired system can take a long time. It might be too late to change the acquisition contract after observing unsatisfactory system tests results. Remember that, during the system design phase, the project team needs to collect data of system tests that have been conducted by the software producer and the existing consumers of the acquired software product. In this implementation phase, the results of these system tests provide data of justification for the acquisition.

## 6.2. System Construction for Systems Construction Development

As discussed earlier in this textbook, nowadays the system in-house construction development strategy is used only for cutting-edge information technology companies, software producers, or large organizations with special and unique requirements. To complete the concept of systems analysis and design, we briefly discuss the major areas that are relevant to system implementation for systems construction, and explain why systems construction is not an option for ordinary business organizations in the modern information technology era.

### 6.2.1. Database construction and tests

The system development team and the database administrator must select a database management system (DBMS), such as ORACLE, IBM DB2, MySQL, Microsoft SQL Server, and Microsoft Access, for the system. The selected DBMS is the tool to construct the database for the system based on the database design specifications. The DBMS will also support the database access and data processing through independent application computer programs. The database construction process includes creating data tables, creating relationships between the tables, creating constraints on the tables and the relationships, deploying data tables in distributed database cases, entering data to the database or converting the current data sources into the database, and writing database programs (i.e., SQL) to support data access and data processing. Finally, an extensive testing process must be conducted to ensure the quality of the database.

### 6.2.2. Application software construction, installation, and tests

The system development team and the programmers must select computer languages that are used to write the application programs. The computer programs are supposed to implement the programs design specifications to meet the system requirements. These computer programs will process the inputs to the system, access the database, and produce the required outputs for the users. Computer programs must go through extensive and time consuming testing processes.

### 6.2.3. Hardware and network installation

The hardware and networking technicians install purchased hardware (e.g., servers, PCs, printers, etc.) and networking equipments (gateway, routers, hubs, etc.). Hardware and network installation activities for system construction development are similar to that for systems acquisition development.

### 6.2.4. Data conversion

In systems construction development data conversion from the current format to the new format for the to-be system can be easier in comparison with systems acquisition development if the systems designers take this task into account when selecting the DBMS and computer programming languages.

### 6.2.5. System tests for constructed system

After rigorous tests of the individual parts (i.e., the database and the computer programs), the constructed software product shall have limited errors. System tests cover many different types of tests beyond the level of individual programs. The principles of **system tests** for a constructed system is the same as that of system tests for an acquired system, but the tests procedure for an in-house developed system should be more extensive since no one really has practically used the system before the system tests.

**User acceptance tests (UAT)** are the final stage of the system development before the new system officially operates. **Alpha testing** is simulated or actual operational testing by selected potential users. The version of the system for alpha testing is called the alpha version, and could still contain flaws. **Beta testing** comes after alpha testing. The version of the constructed system for beta testing is called the beta version, which contains no major errors and is almost ready for full operation. The beta version of the system can be available to a maximal number of future users to use with real operational conditions.

## 6.3. Transition from As-Is System to To-Be System

When the to-be system passes the system tests, the system development team prepares a transition plan to convert the as-is system to the to-be system. A system transition plan includes the following major activities.

- Setting new policies and procedures for the new system.
- Selecting system conversion method.
- Determining a contingency plan in case the conversion fails.
- Scheduling user training.
- Establishing system support facilities.
- Handing-over to the system operation team.

## 6.3.1. New policies and procedures for the new system

Usually, the new system introduces many changes of policies and procedures for the organization. The document of new policies and procedures for the new system must be released before the system transition. It includes the following major components.

- Descriptions of the new policies and procedures.

- Rationale of the new policies and procedures.
- "Roadmap" for directions and steps that users can follow to carry out the new procedures.
- Users responsibilities and consequences of violation of the new policies and procedures.
- Pointers to help assistance.

### 6.3.2. System conversion methods and contingency plans

**System conversion** refers to the process that the new to-be system starts-up and the old system is shut-down. There are three typical system conversion methods: direct conversion, parallel conversion, and phased conversion, as illustrated in Figure 6.1.

In **direct conversion** the new system replaces the old system instantly. Direct conversion is simple, but is risky in case the conversion fails for some reasons. Thus, direct conversion is applied to small and simple information systems.

Using the **parallel conversion** method, both the old system and the new system run simultaneously for a time period until the new system performs stably. A parallel conversion reduces risks caused by a conversion failure, but adds operational costs for the organization.

For a large information system, the **phased conversion** method is often applied. In phased conversion the new system replaces the old system gradually in the phase-out style. The phases in a system conversion operation can be physical locations. For example, a bank might select pilot branches to use the new system first. If the pilot branches succeed, then other branches are converted to the new system. The phases can also be functional areas. For example, a retail company might decide that the inventory management uses the new system first, the shipping management follows, and then other functional areas are converted to the new system. The phased conversion method reduces risks of failure, but it usually takes a relatively long time for the whole conversion process.

The system conversion exposes the organization to **risk** associated with problems in the system conversion. Business operations of the organization might be interrupted by a failure of system conversion, especially when the directed conversion method is applied. The system development team must assess the risk involved, and prepare a **contingency plan** to reduce the risk. The following major concerns must be addressed by a contingency plan.

• What problems could occur during the conversion;

• The conditions, the likelihood, and the consequences of these problems; and

• How the organization can prevent major business disruptions if problems occur during the conversion.

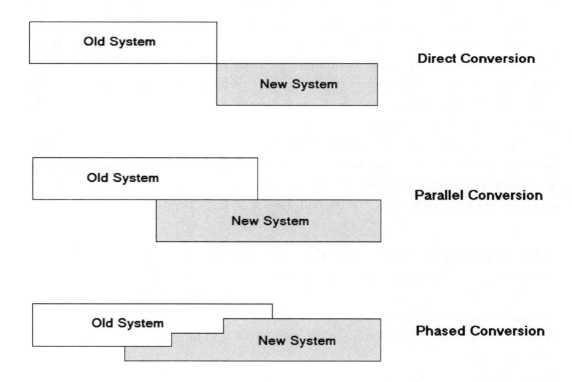

**Figure 6.1. System Conversion Methods**

### 6.3.3. User training

**User training** is a necessary program even before the system conversion. In general, there are two types of users: technical users and end-users, although the two types of users often overlap in many cases. **Technical users** are people who are responsible for the maintenance and operation of the system after the new system starts. For instance, the support team members of information technology department are technical users. **End-users** are non-technical people who use the system but are not responsible for the problems of the system. For instance, CEO, line managers, clerks, and customers are end-users. User training consumes resources of the trainers and the trainees, and is expensive.

If the system is developed by using commercial software products, usually the vendors provide user training for the technical users, and then the technical users train the end-users. If the system is developed through in-house construction, the development team has to train the technical users if the technical users are not the part of the development team.

There are many ways of end-user training. Trainer office visit is used for high-level managerial end-user training. Classroom training is used for a large group of end-users with similar interests. Online demos and tutorials can reach a wide range of end-users and can be effective for end-users with basic needs.

### 6.4. Establishing System Support Facilities and System Hand-Over

The new system must provide **user support** which means helping the end-users to use the system effectively. Common system support facilities include
● online frequently asked questions (FAQs);
● online documents (operation manuals, references, and tutorials);
● online help;
● telephone help desk;
● problem reporting channel, specific support team members for handling problems, and maintenance work orders.

At the end of the system implementation phase, the system development team officially hands-over the system to the **system operations-maintenance team** which is responsible for day-to-day operations, system support, and maintenance of the new system.

## 6.5. Systems Implementation Reports

The deliverables of the system implementation phase include the following items for the documentation.

- System installation records;
- System acceptance tests records;
- System conversion records;
- Reference manuals that describe all specifications of hardware, software (database and computer programs in in-house construction cases), networking of the system, and will be used for system maintenance;
- Operation manuals that describe the operation procedures for the users;
- User training records; and
- Official hand-over document.

## *Key Terms*

Systems implementation phase
Configuring an ERP system
Customization
Data conversion
System tests for acquired system
  Reliability tests
  Functional requirement tests
  Error handling tests
System implementation for system
  construction

User acceptance tests (UAT) for
  constructed system
  Alpha testing
  Beta testing
System conversion
  Direct conversion
  Parallel conversion
  Phased conversion
Risk of conversion
Contingency plan
Technical users

End users

User training

System hand-over

System documentation

Operation manual

References

Tutorials

System implementation reports


## Exercises of Systems Analysis and Design Course Project


1. Discuss the implementation process for the new system of your course project.

2. Specify the method of data conversion that could be used for the new system of your course project.

3. Discuss user training for your course project.

4. Select a system conversion method for your course project.

5. Discuss your plan of system tests for your course project.

6. Discuss the support facilities after the new system starts to operate for your course project.

# CHAPTER 7. SYSTEMS MAINTENANCE

The **systems maintenance phase** improves the new information system. It includes the following major activities.

(1) Management of system support and system maintenance.

(2) Post-project evaluation.

(3) Preparation for the next new information system.

## 7.1. Management of User Support and System Maintenance

An information system is usually not perfect. The users might experience difficulties in using the new system. Also, requests for changes to meet additional business requirements often occur frequently.

### 7.1.1. User support

If the system was developed by using a commercialized software product, the vendor of the software product can provide user training and helping the users. However, if the system is large, a support group (i.e., technical users) might be needed to help the users in the day-to-day operations. The support group members possess good knowledge of the commercialized software product, and can help the users promptly. The support group has a close connection with the technical team of the vendor or the software producer to solve complex problems.

If the system was constructed in-house, the user training and helping are carried out by an internal support team. The organization of support team for a large in-house constructed information system could be large.

### 7.1.2. System maintenance procedure

**System maintenance** refers to an activity that makes changes to the system in response to new business needs or reported deficiency of the system. Generally, there are several types of system maintenance.

● **Corrective maintenance**: Reactive modification of the system to correct discovered errors. The correction of a computer program bug is a typical example of corrective maintenance.

- **Adaptive maintenance**: Modification of the system in response to the changing environment. For example, the system maintenance team makes changes to the computer programs when the state sales tax rate increases.

- **Perfective maintenance**: Modification of the system to improve the performance or maintainability. For example, in response to the customers' complain that the online sales system does not show the shipping costs until reaching the check-out point, the maintenance team makes changes to the Web site so that a hyperlink of the shipping cost schedule is included in the home page.

- **Preventive maintenance**: Modification of the system to prevent possible damages. For instance, to prevent unauthorized access to the system, the mainten-ance team makes changes to the password registration and authorization rules.

For a system with a commercialized software product, system maintenance is carried out by the software producer. For an in-house constructed system, system maintenance is a major task of the system support and maintenance team. In any cases, the organization should have a formal system maintenance procedure to handle complains or requests systematically and promptly. Generally, a system **maintenance procedure** includes the following processes.

(1) The user or the help desk experiences a problem, or a maintenance team member perceives a necessary change, files a request for changes, and sends the request to the system support and maintenance team manager.

(2) The maintenance team analyzes the request and checks its validity. It develops a maintenance solution to the problem or rejects the request for changes.

(3) The maintenance job takes place. It is carried out by the producer of the software product if the problem is caused by the acquired software product, or is carried out by the maintenance team if the system was constructed in-house.

(4) The maintenance team works with the users to test the result of maintenance to ensure that the problem has been solved.

The general system maintenance procedure is depicted in Figure 7.1.

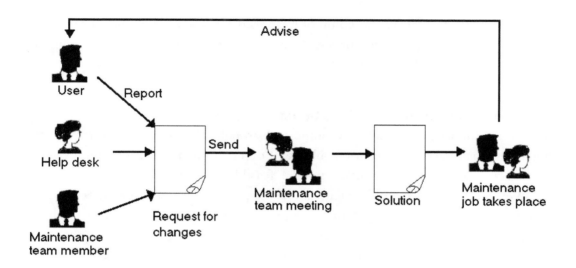

**Figure 7.1. General System Maintenance Procedure**

## 7.2. Post-Project Evaluation

After a certain time period of operation of the new system, the system management team should conduct **post-project evaluation** to assess the quality of the development project. A post-project evaluation examines whether the system development project has achieved its objectives using metrics. Metrics are a set of measurements for assessing the project outcomes. The **metrics** for post-project evaluation include:

- the planned system scope and the actual system scope;
- the expected functional requirements and the actual system functionalities;
- the expected nonfunctional requirements and the actual system features;
- the users' satisfaction;
- the overall system usability;
- the overall system efficiency performance, and
- the expected financial performance and the actual financial performance.

Surveys and interviews are commonly applied methods for post-project evaluation. A post-project evaluation process contributes to the organizational learning for the next information system project.

## 7.3. Preparation for the Next New System

System maintenance consumes resources. Naturally, the older the system is, the higher the maintenance expenses would be. For a computerized information system, especially a large system, it might not be feasible to throw the old system away completely. A part of the old system can be integrated into the potential new system and will become a **legacy system**. A legacy system is an old system or a part of computer applications that continues to be used because it still functions, even though newer technology or more efficient and effective methods of performing the needed applications are currently available. The reason of keeping a legacy system is to save the development and replacement costs. However, the maintenance of a legacy system could be difficult and costly in the long run.

To prepare for the next generation information system, the system maintenance team retains important information of the current system such as

● long standing problems of the system;

● maintenance costs of the system;

● performance records of the system in comparison with similar systems in the industry; and

● the potential legacy system for the next generation information system of the organization.

Once the system maintenance costs reach to high, and the performance of the system becomes relative inferior given the advances of new information technology, a new information system project is to be initiated and the SDLC starts a new cycle.

## *Key Terms*

| | |
|---|---|
| Systems maintenance phase | System maintenance management |
| Corrective maintenance | System maintenance procedure |
| Adaptive maintenance | Legacy system |
| Perfective maintenance | Post-project evaluation |
| Preventive maintenance | Metrics for post-project evaluation |
| User support | Preparation for the next new system |

## *Exercises of Systems Analysis and Design Course Project*

1. Discuss the user support issues for the new system of your course project.

2. Discuss the system maintenance issues for the new system of your course project.

3. Discuss how you would conduct a post-project evaluation for your course project.

4. Discuss how you would collect information for the long-term consideration of system development in the organization after the new system of your course project starts to operate.

# APPENDIX A. GUIDELINE FOR SYSTEMS ACQUISITION PROJECTS

## 1. Project Scheme

The project include systems analysis phase and systems design phase for systems acquisition.

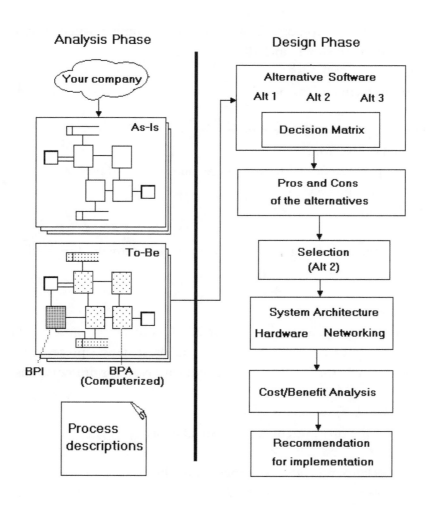

## 2. Learning Objective of the Project

The learning objective of the project is to analyze and design a computerized information system for a small/medium business organization. The company must be real and approachable. Small business with little support of computerized information system is ideal for this project.

## 3. Project Proposal

This project is a group project. Each group must submit a typed proposal by the deadline. The proposal should include:

(1) Title page:
   List of group members (names).
   Title of the project.
(2) Problem / opportunities description:
   Background of the firm.
   Problems/opportunities with business requirements and business processes.
   Objective of the project.
(3) Context diagram.

The approved proposal, along with the instructor's comments (no grading), will be returned to each group a week after.

## 4. Project Presentations

Each group gives two presentations. The first presentation presents the systems analysis result for your project, and the second presentation presents the systems design result for your project. PowerPoint slides are used for presentations.

### 4.1. Presentation-1: Systems analysis

The guideline for the first presentation is listed below.

(1) The firm's background and an overview of the business. [1 minute]
(2) General overview of the problems / opportunities for the firm to improve the business process. [1.5 minute]

(3) Constraints (budget, time, human resource, current hardware/software ...) [1.5 minute]

(4) The scope of the course project (the part of the business process you are going to investigate). Show and explain the context diagram. [1 minute]

(5) The As-Is system of the information system related to the business processes you are investigating. [5 minutes]

    (5.1) Context diagram (logical) - the general context of the business

    (5.2) Level-1 diagram (logical) - major business processes

    (5.3) Level-2 diagrams - detailed business processes

(6) The To-Be system of the information system to improve the business processes. [4 minutes]

    (6.1) Context diagram (logical) - it may or may not be the same as (5.1)

    (6.2) Level-1 diagram (logical) - it may or may not be the same as (5.2)

    (6.3) Level-2 diagrams - Some of these diagrams (logical or physical) must be different from (5.3)

    (6.4) Indicate the difference between the As-Is system and To-Be system.

(7) Summarize the differences between the As-Is system and the To-Be system, and explain why the change will solve the problems or catch opportunities you identified. [1 minute]

(8) The objectives of your project and general prospective solutions. [1 minute]

### 4.2. Presentation-2: Systems Design

The guideline for the final presentation is listed below.

(1) A quick refreshing the company's background and problems/opportunities identified. [1minute]

(2) A quick overview of the business process: As-Is system and To-Be system (using the DFDs) and highlight the differences between the As-Is and To-Be systems. [1.5 minutes]

(3) Constraints (budget, time, human resource ...) and an overview of computer solutions. [0.5 minute]

(4) Three alternative application software products. For each alternative:

(4.1) Overview and sample screenshots of user interface that are pertinent to the processes you modeled and other system requirements

(4.2) Justification of the alternative for the system requirements and constraints

(4.3) Summary and comparison of the alternatives (pros and cons)

(4.4) Decision matrices (Functional and non-functional) [6 minutes]

(5) System architecture - hardware and networking (You may have alternatives system architecture designs) [0.5 minute]

(6) Cost/benefit analysis:

(Read Chapter 3 and the spreadsheet in Figure 3.1. Use NPV for ROI and break-even. An integrated spreadsheet covers the following items.)

(6.1) Cost:

- Tangible costs

  - Development costs: hardware, networking (all components and ISP), software, installation, data conversion, training, etc.

  - Operational costs: leasing, utilities, maintenance, etc.

- Intangible costs

  - Risks, etc.

(6.2) Benefit:

- Tangible benefits: manpower saving, office supplies saving, increase sales, reduce losses, etc.

- Intangible benefits: quality service, improve work condition, etc.

(6.3) Cost/benefit analysis models (spreadsheet)

- Cash flow analysis, Return on investment, break even model [4 minutes]

(7) Recommendations of implementation for the firm

- Recommendations

- Time frame

- Training

- Installation and data conversion

- System conversion

- Follow-up activities, etc. [2 minutes]

### *4.3. Project Report*

Each group must submit a project report. The report text should be no longer than 15 pages, 1.5 spaced (exclusive of the title page, diagrams, process descriptions, matrices, and appendices which have no limit). All diagrams should be computer drawing. The report must include the following items.

(1) Title page
- The title of the project
- Group members
- Date

(2) Text
- Introduction
- System requirements overview
- System analysis (As-Is system and To-Be system)
- System design
  - Alternative application software products
  - Decision matrices
  - System architecture - networking and hardware
- Cost/benefit analysis
- Recommendations and implementation plan

(3) Diagrams or matrices if not in the text

(4) Process descriptions

(5) Appendices (no page limitation)
- Samples of As-Is business processes
- Samples of user interface screenshots that demonstrate the features of the user interface of the alternative application software packages that match to the business process, data, and non-functional requirements.
- Information sources of the computer software, hardware, networking, and vendors
- Any other useful information

# APPENDIX B. CASE TOOL: VISIBLE ANALYST *

## 1. CASE Tools

**CASE** (**Computer Aided Systems Engineering** or **Computer Aided Software Engineering**) tools are a category of software that supports the information systems development process. The support functions of CASE tools vary depending on the product, ranging from project management to systems diagramming and validation, and even to generating interim prototypes of database and computer code.

The central component of a CASE tool is the **CASE repository** that stores all the diagrams and project information, and is shared by all project team members. The CASE repository ensures the project components consistent. A CASE tool has become a necessary instrument for an information system development project because of the advantages in the following aspects.

• A CASE tool can be used to coordinate the project team activities, and to facilitate knowledge sharing among the project team members.

• A CASE tool allows the project team to follow the standard terminology, the same procedures, the same names of the system components, and the same format of documentation. Thus, the standards of the new system can be created and be enforced through the CASE tool.

• A CASE tool is not just a computer drawing tool. It can have intelligent features to verify the systems analysis and design results to a certain degree, and to eliminate the syntax errors in the data flow diagrams (DFD). Thus, a CASE tool can reduce errors in the systems development process.

• A CASE tool can generate consistent documents with detailed information for each phase of the SDLC. Thus, a CASE tool can make the systems development process more efficient.

---

* **Acknowledgement:** Mr. John Nash and Mr. Russell Abisla at Visible Systems Corporation have provided their kind help and valuable suggestions for this tutorial. This tutorial is permitted by Visible Systems Corporation.

149

## 2. Visible Analyst

Visible Analyst, a product of Visible Systems Corporation, is a CASE tool. It has been widely used in many industrial organizations as well as educational institutions. There are many modules in Visible Analyst that support various modeling techniques across the systems analysis and design phases.

This textbook uses the data flow diagram (DFD) part for business process modeling. This tutorial demonstrates how Visible Analyst can be used for your systems analysis and design project in an efficient and effective way. The objectives of this tutorial for students are:

(1) Be able use a CASE tool for business process modeling for systems analysis.

(2) Be able to contrast the as-is system and the to-be system using DFD for systems design.

(3) Understand the advantages of CASE tools in general.

The rest part of this appendix is a step-by-step practice demonstration.

## A. Login

Visible Analysis can be installed on the server of the computing lab. The menu for the access of Visible Analysis depends on the lab setting, and the instructor shall be able to know. The logon IDs are set up as Project Manager level users so that they can access their specific project.

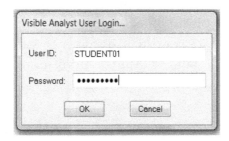

## B. File menu

The File menu allows the user to create a new project, to select the project in progress, to view the activities of the project, to open diagrams of the project.

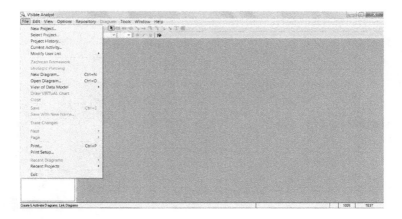

## C. Creating a new project

The user types the name of the new project, selects Data Flow for the systems analysis and design method, and chooses Gane & Sarson for the DFD style.

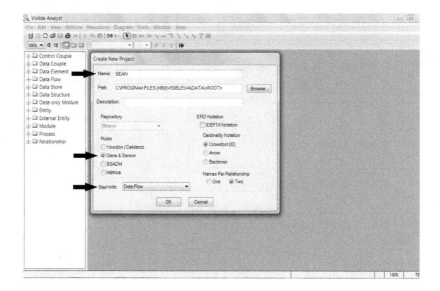

## D. Creating a DFD

You must start from a Context Diagram for your project. Make sure you click on the checkbox.

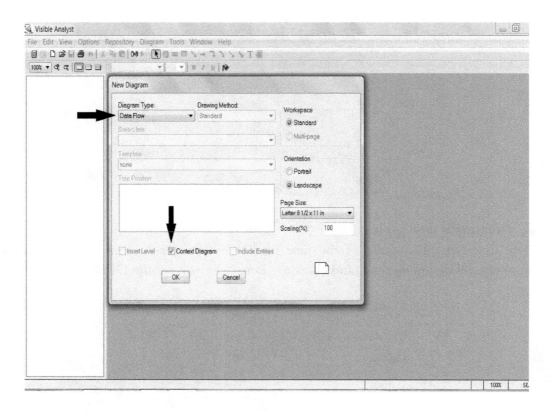

## E. Using symbols of DFD

Use diagram symbols on the top menu to draw the context diagram. You may re-shape the symbols you created. Use unique name for each symbol.

*Process:*

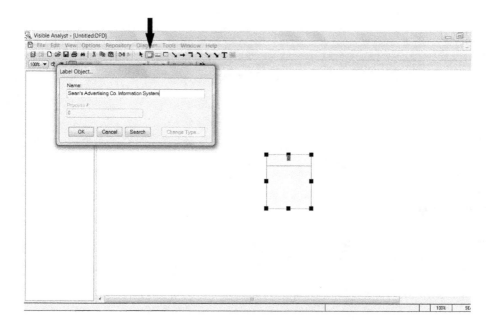

(Process - cont'd)

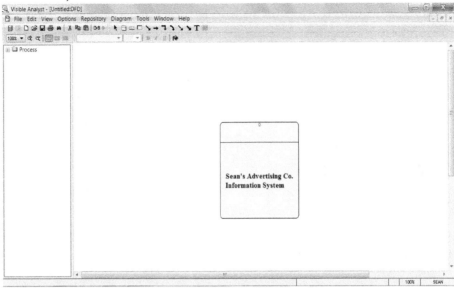

*External Entity:*

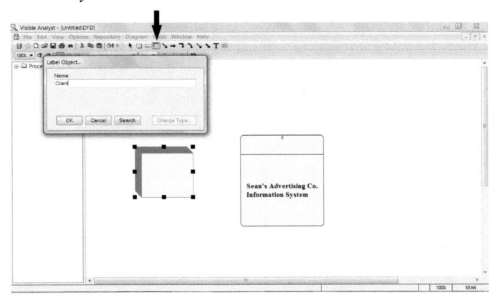

## Data Flow:

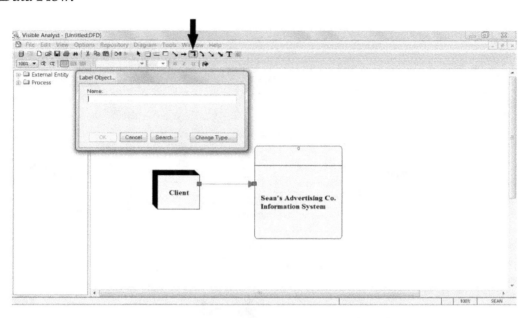

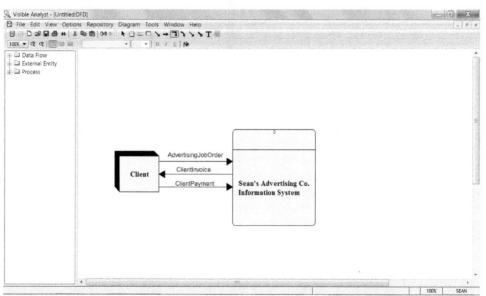

(Data Flow - cont'd)

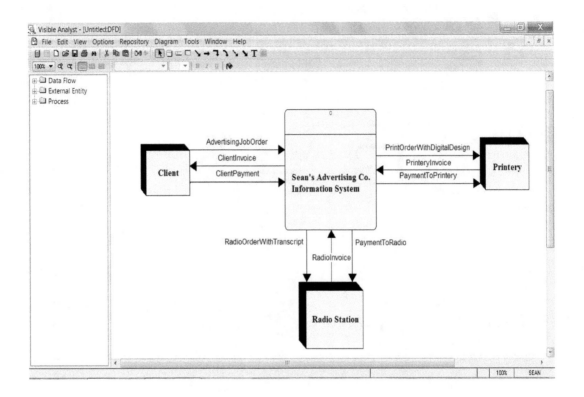

### Data Store:

A context diagram does not contain any data store. In the Level-1 DFD, you will add data stores.

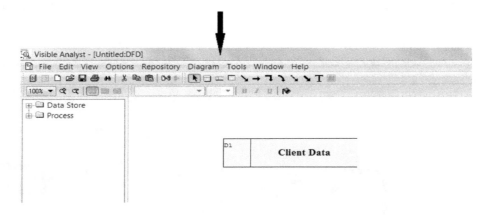

## F. Saving the context diagram

Before you go further for your project, you must save the context diagram first.

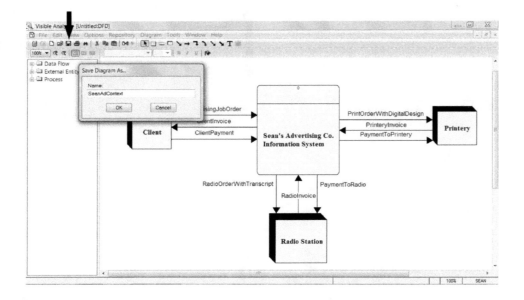

## G. Decomposition

To decompose the context diagram into new DFD at Level-1, right mouse click on the process symbol. Choose **Explode**. In Visible Analyst, "Explode" means "decompose." Explode can be used decompose a process at any level (e.g., from Level-0 to Level-1, and then from Level-1 to Level-2).

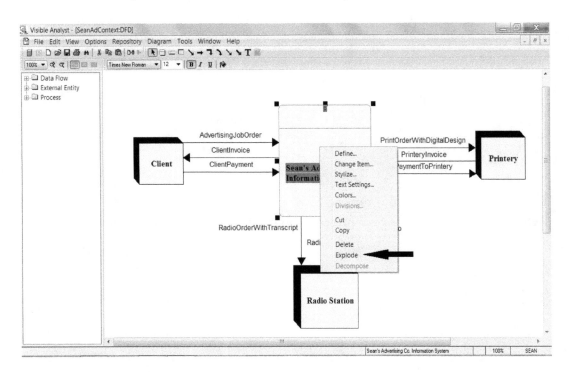

(Decomposition - cont'd)

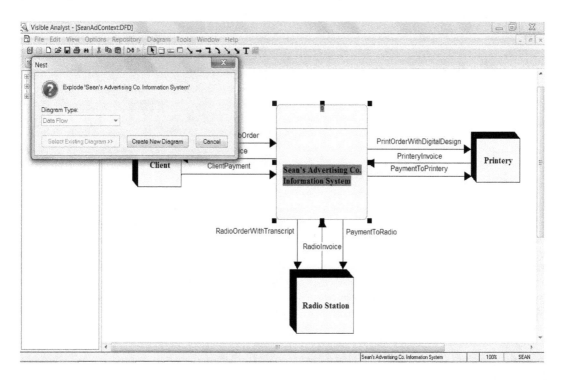

The CASE tool enforces the balancing between the context diagram and the Level-1 DFD by carrying on the data flows from the context diagram to the new Level-1 DFD. If a warning message alerts that there are many data flows for the screen, move some of the flows to the middle of the diagram, and re-explode the parent process. All data flows are dragged down to the new child diagram.

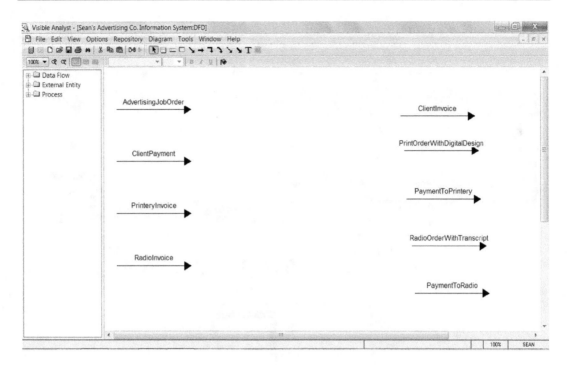

Visible Analyst, however, does not automatically drag down the entities to the new child diagram. The user has the responsibility to add all entities on the Level-1 DFD, and re-arrange the layout of these data flows, as shown in the next screenshot.

If you find some data flows were lost, you may go back to the context diagram and re-explode it to bring all data flows back. You can also delete and redraw a data flow, but keep the same data flow name as shown in the context diagram.

You may want to save the intermediate result from time to time in order not to lose all you have done when the computer crashes for some reasons.

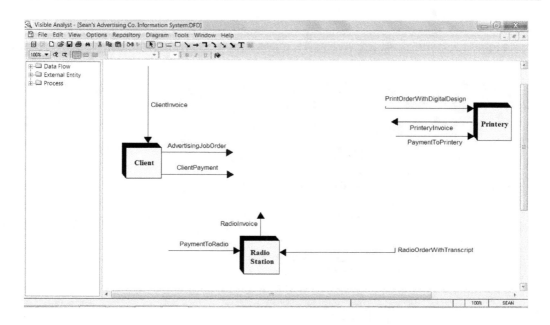

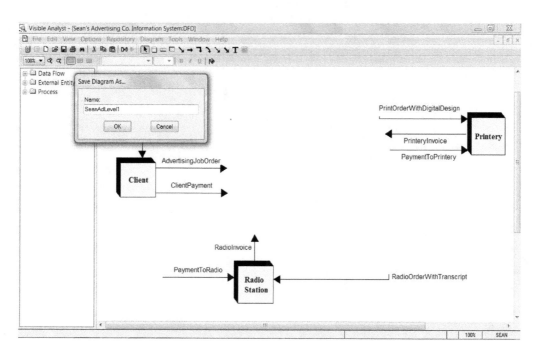

If you click on the File menu, you can have the open diagrams window.

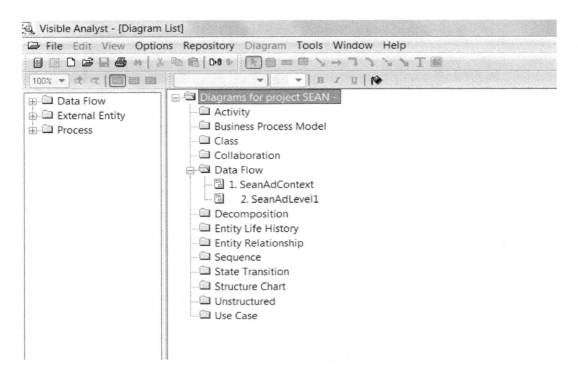

## H. Verifying diagrams

Visible Analyst possesses powerful features of DFD verification. Click on Diagram on the top menu, select **Analyze** on the pull-down menu, the user is able to verify the diagram or the entire project to find out syntax errors. If the CASE tool does not detect any syntax error, it displays the OK message. Note that the Analyzer of Visible Analyst enforces two-way balancing.

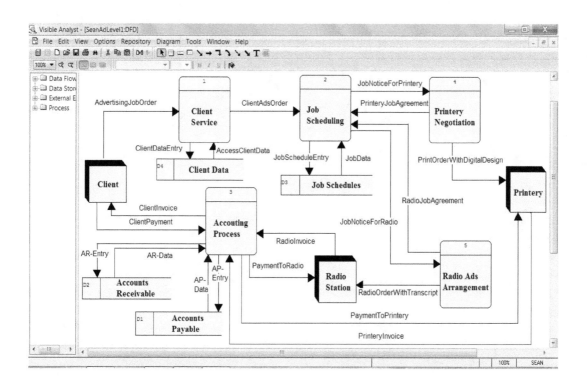

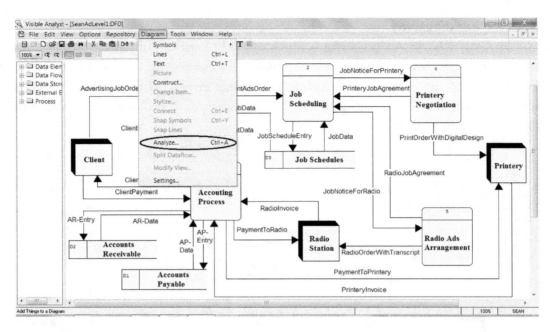

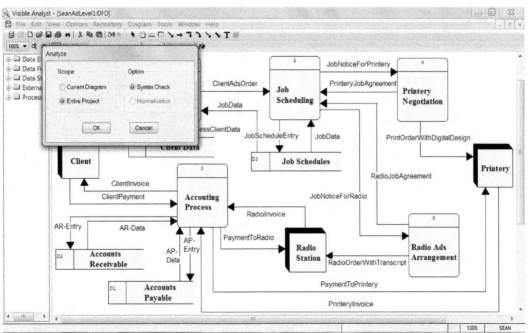

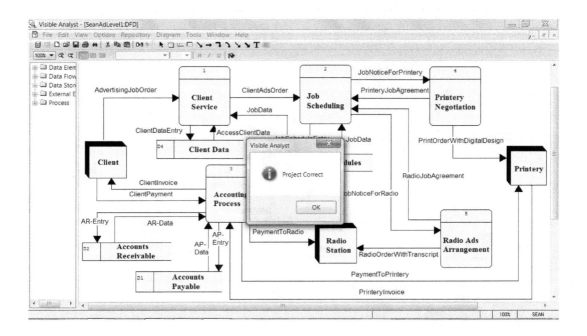

If the DFDs violate rules and contain syntax errors, the CASE tool will display error messages. Interpretation of error messages is not an easy task, but the error message would indicate the location of errors.

## I. Defining entities, data flows, data stores, and processes

Double click on a diagram symbol or line to access the item's Define Item pane. Of course, each type of item has its unique the structure of the Define Item pane.

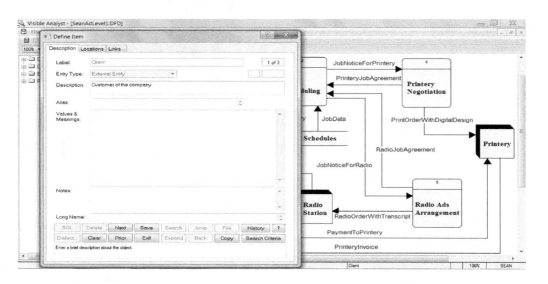

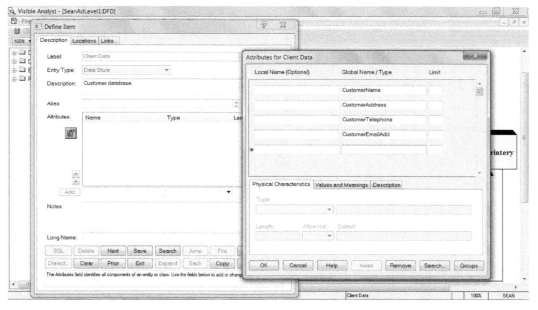

Process descriptions:

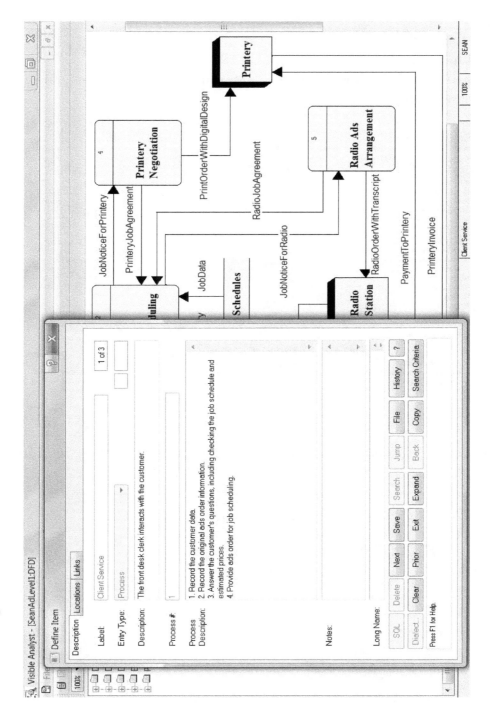

## J. Repository

The CASE tool keeps every piece of information about the project in the repository, as shown in the following screenshot.

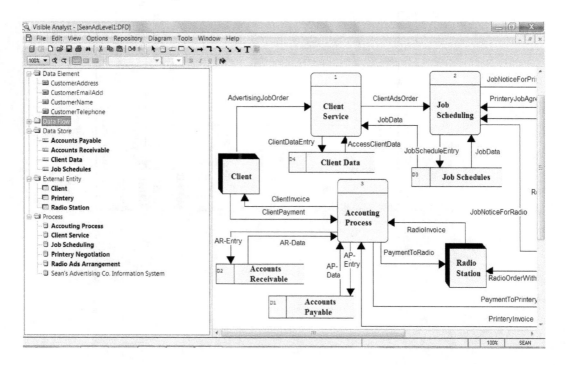

## K. Color

There are many other functions in Visible Analyst. The use of color could be very useful to compare the DFDs. The following screenshots show the use of the Color function for the Client Service process.

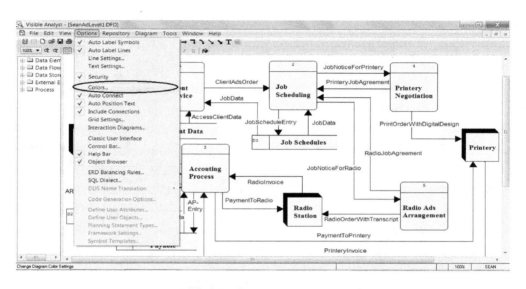

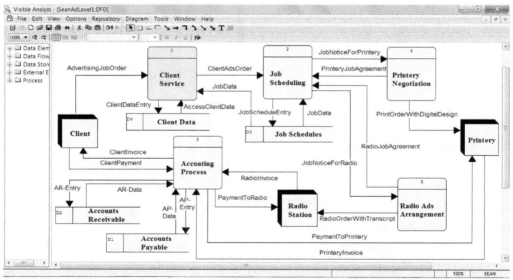

## L. View

The user is allowed to change the way of displays using the View menu. However, a misuse of some menu items (e.g., Show Line Names) could confuse the user.

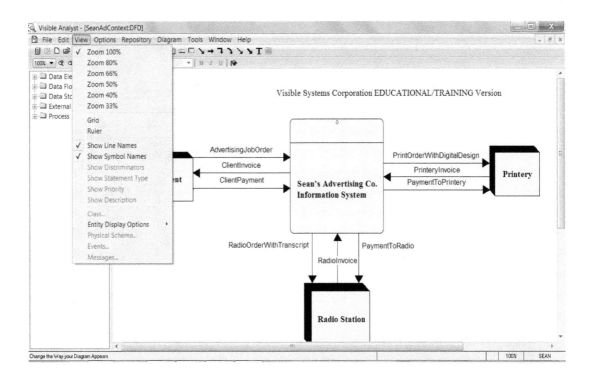

## M. Copy-pasting diagrams

The user might want to copy-paste diagrams to reduce the duplication work when developing DFDs for the as-is system and the to-be system, and also to make the contrast between the two set of DFDs clear. To make a copy-paste operation for two sets of DFDs, you must create two separate projects, say, AS-IS and TO-BE. Use the following steps, assuming the user wants to copy diagrams from the AS-IS project to the TO-BE project.

- Open the context DFD diagram of AS-IS.
- Choose Edit on the top menu, and then choose Select All on the pull-down menu to enclose all diagram lines and symbols within a bounding box.
- Choose Edit on the top menu, and then Copy to copy the diagram to the Windows clipboard. Nothing happens on the screen.
- Create a new project (TO-BE) using the same DFD Rule set.
- Create a new Context DFD in the TO-BE project, and type a name for the process, say, TOBE. This process name is automatically added to a context level diagram.
- Save the diagram with a name, say, TOBE-Context.
- Right mouse click on the process TOBE, and choose Delete on the pop-up menu.
- Save the diagram again.
- Choose Edit on the top menu, and then choose Paste on the pull-down menu. The AS-IS context diagram is pasted onto the TOBE-Context diagram.
- Save the diagram again.
- Right mouse click on the TOBE process, and the Explode option is enabled which allows you to decompose the context diagram.
- Repeat the above procedure for the Level-1 DFD and Level-2 DFDs.
- After two identical sets of DFDs are created, it is possible to add, delete, or color any symbols in the DFDs of the TO-BE project.

All of the symbols and lines (data flows) will have their repository entries created when the diagram is saved. However, the data elements in the AS-IS project are NOT included in the TO-BE project during the paste operation. In other words, the repository will not have the data elements for the TO-BE project, and the user must re-enter the pertinent data elements for the TO-BE project.

## N. Backup and Restore

The user is allowed to backup and restore the project by using the Tools menu.

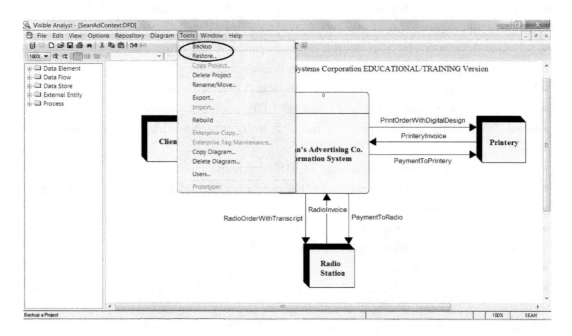

# APPENDIX C. AN EXAMPLE OF SYSTEMS ANALYSIS AND DESIGN *

(Note: This case example describes key components of systems analysis and design for systems acquisition development. It is not a complete project report. A detailed guideline of course project is exhibited in Appendix A.)

## Introduction

GreenBay Seafood Inc. is a seafood intermediary company located on the south-east coast of Massachusetts. Three generations make up the backbone of this company; the grandfather works in the back office, two grandsons work on the trading floor, and the father takes care of all. The building where the business operates is relatively small. The company has 6 full time employees. They have worked in this company for at least 4 years. The annual revenue of the company is about 5 million USD.

In the summer and fall, primarily local seafood products are bought from local fisheries and sold to customers worldwide, including many location in the US, Canada, Europe, and South America. In the off-season, seafood products are imported from Canada and Maine and are sold to the regular customers. The company has seafood storage tanks with a capacity of over 20,000 pounds. The customers' orders are packed overnight and shipped on that day in insulated containers to ensure fresh products.

## Problems and Opportunities

Currently, the business processes at GreenBay Seafood are basically manual. The procurement process, receiving process, sales process, and inventory process are all done by hand with papers on the trading floor. Accounting ledgers and payroll process are done in the back office manually in the traditional way.

---

* **Acknowledgement:** The valuable contributions of Mr. Thomas Jacobs, Mr. Joseph Machado, Mr. Michael Boudreau, and Mr. Christopher Azevedo to this case example are gratefully appreciated.

When the grandfather is approaching to retirement, the shareholders are considering the information technology for business processes to renew the company for the next generation.

## System Requirements Overview

### *Functional requirements*

The functional requirements for the information system of GreenBay Seafood can be defined in 5 categories: Sales, Procurement, Receiving, Scheduling and payroll, and Cash flow management, as summarized below.

### (1) Sales

The requirements for the sales business process include
- pricing for the sale of seafood;
- recording and confirming the sales order;
- adjusting the inventory on hand against the confirmed sales order;
- creating an order slip for the sale which will be used for shipping.

### (2) Procurement

The requirements for the procurement business process include
- recording the grading different types of seafood;
- providing dynamic inventory information for negotiating a price with the supplier;
- recording all detailed data of the purchased seafood.

### (3) Receiving

The requirements for the receiving business process include
- tracking the grading and the amount of seafood that is actually received;
- recording the net weight (total weight minus packaging weight) for each package;
- recording the weight of ungraded product which is different from the procurement;
- creating or updating the profile of the supplier.

## (4) Scheduling and payroll

The requirements for the scheduling and payroll business process include

- scheduling the work time for each employee;
- recording the actual work hours of each employee;
- calculating payroll.

## (5) Cash flow management

The requirements for the cash flow management process include

- recording all accounts receivable and accounts payable ledgers;
- maintaining various accounts;
- generating cash flow prediction;
- generating financial statements for the company's owners.

### *Nonfunctional requirements*

The nonfunctional requirements for the information system of GreenBay Seafood can be defined in 5 categories: operational, performance, security, vendor reputation and services, and leasing, as summarized below.

## (1) Usability

- The system must be easy to learn and easy to use for the traditional small business.
- The system is able to integrate the Internet for international trade.

## (2) Performance

- The system must have a sufficient capacity to store necessary information.
- The system must response at an adequate speed for trading.

## (3) Security

- The system must have access control, and protect the company's information.
- The system must have virus protection.
- The system needs capabilities of backup and recovery.

### (4) Vendor

- The vendor who provides the software product must have a good reputation.
- The vendor must provide user training because there is no designated IT person in this company.
- The vendor must sign a maintenance services contract.

### (5) Leasing

- GreenBay Seafood prefers to lease the software product to ease cash flows and to control risks of failure.

### Data Flow Diagrams

Based on the collected information for determining the system requirements, DFDs are generated to specify the functional requirements. Here, only the to-be system Level 2 DFDs are included.

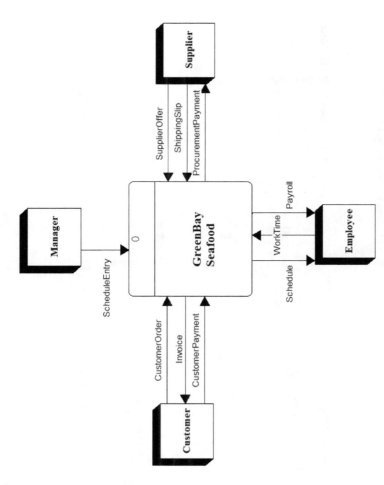

**Figure C-1. Context Diagram of the As-Is System**

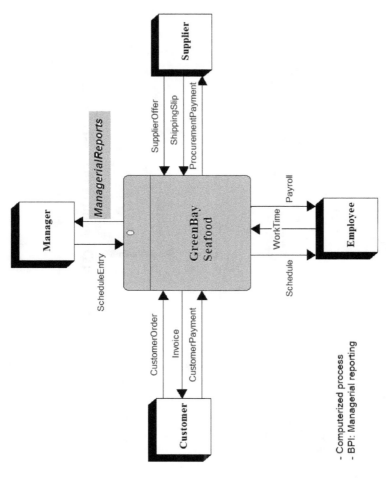

Figure C-2. Context Diagram of the To-Be System

- Computerized process
- BPI: Managerial reporting

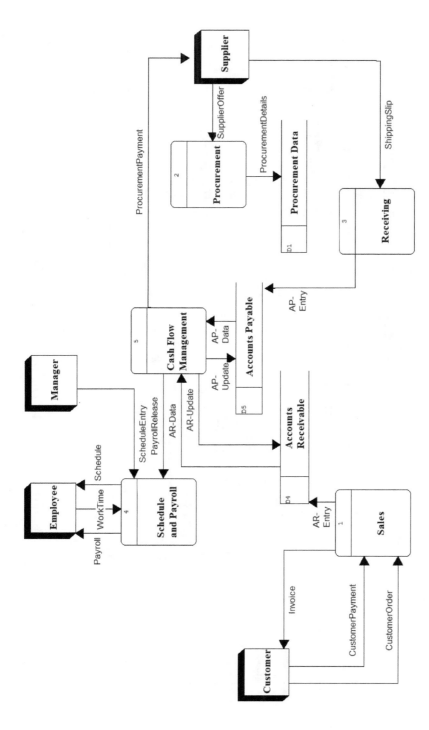

Figure C-3. Level-1 Diagram of the As-Is System

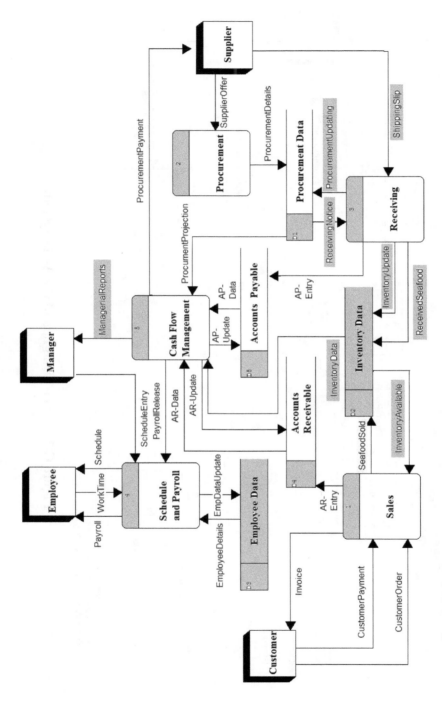

**Figure C-4. Level-1 Diagram of the To-Be System**

- Computerized processes
- Real-time inventory management
- Timely managerial reporting

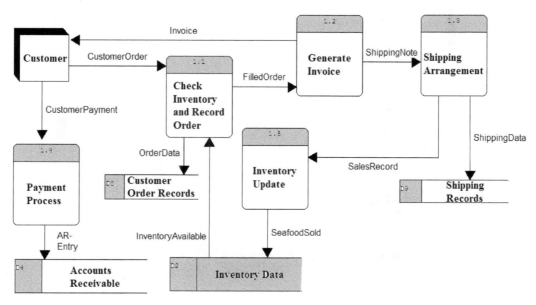

**Figure C-5. Level-2 Diagram of Process-1 (Sales) of the To-Be System**

| Process | Descriptions |
|---|---|
| P1.1.<br>Check Inventory and Record Order | Check the inventory against the customer's order.<br>If the inventory is sufficient<br>   Then record the customer's order<br>Else record the back order and send a notice to the customer. |
| P1.2.<br>Generate Invoice | Estimate the price of the seafood order.<br>Estimate the shipping cost.<br>Generate an invoice for the customer. |
| P1.3.<br>Shipping Arrangement | Generate a shipping order.<br>Record the shipping data.<br>Update the inventory. |
| P1.4.<br>Payment Process | Check the payment against the invoice.<br>Update accounts receivable.<br>Banking the check. |
| P1.5.<br>Inventory Update | Deduct the amount of seafood from the inventory file. |

**Figure C-6. Primitive Process Descriptions for Processes 1.1 - 1.5**

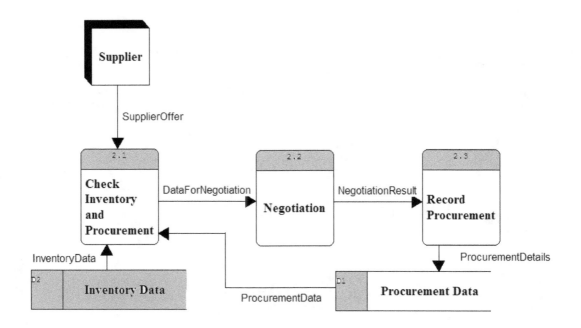

**Figure C-7. Level-2 Diagram of Process-2 (Procurement) of the To-Be System**

| Process | Descriptions |
|---|---|
| P2.1.<br>Check Inventory and Procurement | Check the inventory against the supplier's offer.<br>If the inventory is low<br>  Start negotiation<br>Else decline the offer. |
| P2.2.<br>Negotiation | Negotiate the seafood price.<br>If the price is appropriate<br>  Send a procurement agreement<br>Else decline the offer. |
| P2.3.<br>Record Procurement | Acquire details of the supplier's offer.<br>Record the data to the procurement file. |

**Figure C-8. Primitive Process Descriptions for Processes 2.1 - 2.3**

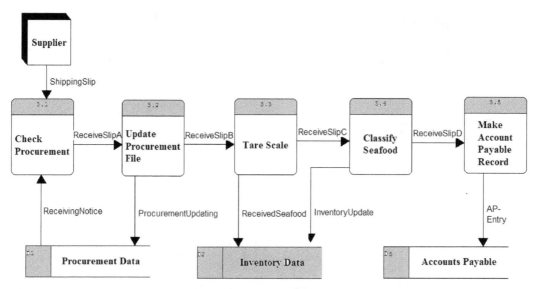

**Figure C-9. Level-2 Diagram of Process-3 (Receiving) of the To-Be System**

| Process | Descriptions |
|---|---|
| P3.1.<br>Check Procurement | Retrieve the procurement record against the shipping slip.<br>Check the procurement record.<br>Find any disparity between the shipping slip and the procurement record. |
| P3.2.<br>Update Procurement File | Include the shipping slip data into the procurement file.<br>Record the disparity. |
| P3.3.<br>Tare Scale | Weight the shipped seafood.<br>Deduct tank's weight.<br>Weight data are recorded to the inventory database in real-time. |
| P3.4.<br>Classify Seafood | Measure the seafood product.<br>Record the class data to the inventory database. |
| P3.5.<br>Make Accounts Payable Record | Calculate the cost of the received seafood product.<br>Create an accounts payable record for the supplier. |

**Figure C-10. Primitive Process Descriptions for Processes 3.1 - 3.5**

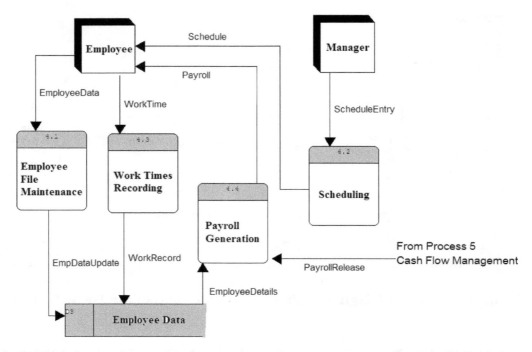

**Figure C-11. Level-2 Diagram of Process-4 (Schedule and Payroll) of the To-Be System**

| Process | Descriptions |
|---------|--------------|
| P4.1. Employee File Maintenance | Record the employee profile. Update the employee profile if there is a change. |
| P4.2. Work Times Recording | Record the work hours daily for each employee. |
| P4.3. Payroll Generation | Upon the release of payroll and bonus, Calculate payroll for each employee. Write checks for each employee. |
| P4.4. Scheduling | Manager enters scheduling data. Advise the schedule to each employee. |

**Figure C-12. Primitive Process Descriptions for Processes 4.1 - 4.4**

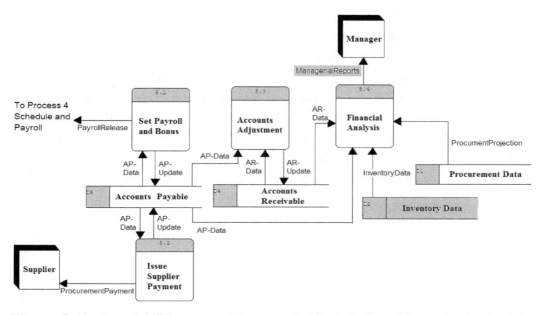

**Figure C-13. Level-2 Diagram of Process-5 (Cash Follow Management) of the To-Be System**

| Process | Descriptions |
|---------|--------------|
| P5.1. Set Payroll and Bonus | Check accounts payable and accounts receivable. Set a limit for payroll and bonus. |
| P5.2. Issue Supplier Payment | Check accounts payable and accounts receivable. Write a check for a due payment for supplier. |
| P5.3. Accounts Adjustment | Record expenses or income other than sales or procurement. |
| P5.4. Financial Analysis | Check accounts payable and accounts receivable. Generate daily and weekly cash flow projection. Check the inventory and procurement data. Generate financial statements. Generate customer sales and payment analysis reports. Generate inventory analysis reports. Generate procurement analysis reports. |

**Figure C-14. Primitive Process Descriptions for Processes 5.1 - 5.4**

**System Architecture Design**

The building of GreenBay Seafood is old, and wiring is not an option. A wireless network will be used for the to-be system. A desktop and a small printer will be set in the back office to process inventory, cash flows, scheduling, and procurement. A desktop and an industrial digital scale will be set on the trading floor to process receiving and sales. There will be a wireless barcode scanner for tracking tanks and containers. The wireless network is controlled be a wireless router, and is linked to the Internet through a DSL modem provided by Verizon, a local Internet service provider. The overall design of the system architecture is exhibited in Figure C-15.

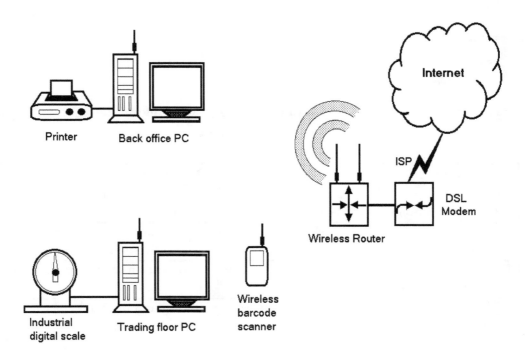

**Figure C-15. System Architecture Design for GreenBay Seafood Inc.**

## Decision Matrices

Figure C-16 and Figure C-17 exhibit the decision matrices for evaluation of software products for GreenBay Seafood. These two decision matrices can be used for exercise.

| Functionality | Weight | MS Dynamics | inFlow * | SIMBA ‡ |
|---|---|---|---|---|
| **P1. Sales** | - | - | - | - |
| P1.1. Check Inventory and Record Order | | | | |
| P1.2. Generate Invoice | | | | |
| P1.3. Shipping Arrangement | | | | |
| P1.4. Payment Process | | | | |
| P1.5. Inventory Update | | | | |
| **P2. Procurement** | - | - | - | - |
| P2.1. Check Inventory and Procurement | | | | |
| P2.2. Negotiation | | | | |
| P2.3. Record Procurement | | | | |
| **P3. Receiving** | - | - | - | - |
| P3.1. Check Procurement | | | | |
| P3.2. Update Procurement File | | | | |
| P3.3. Tare Scale | | | | |
| P3.4. Classify Seafood | | | | |
| P3.5. Make Accounts Payable Record | | | | |
| **P4. Schedule and Payroll** | - | - | - | - |
| P4.1. Employee File Maintenance | | | | |
| P4.2. Work Times Recording | | | | |
| P4.3. Payroll Generation | | | | |
| P4.4. Scheduling | | | | |
| **P5. Cash Follow Management** | - | - | - | - |
| P5.1. Set Payroll and Bonus | | | | |
| P5.2. Issue Supplier Payment | | | | |
| P5.3. Accounts Adjustment | | | | |
| P5.4. Financial Analysis | | | | |
| **Total Scores** | - | | | |

* http://www.inflowinventory.com/      ‡ http://fishlabels.com/

**Figure C-16. Decision Matrix of Functional Requirements for the GreenBay Seafood Example**

| Non-Functional Requirements | Weight | MS Dynamics | inFlow | SIMBA |
|---|---|---|---|---|
| **1. Usability** | - | - | - | - |
| 1.1. Easy to use - Quality of the user interface design | | | | |
| 1.2. Integration to the Internet | | | | |
| **2. Performance** | - | - | - | - |
| 2.1. Capacity of data storage | | | | |
| 2.2. Adequate speed for fast trading | | | | |
| **3. Security** | - | - | - | - |
| 3.1. Access control | | | | |
| 3.2. Virus protection | | | | |
| 3.4. Capacity of backup and recovery | | | | |
| **4. Vendor** | - | - | - | - |
| 4.1. Reputation | | | | |
| 4.2. User training service | | | | |
| 4.3. Contract of maintenance | | | | |
| **5. Leasing** | - | - | - | - |
| 5.1. Leasing | | | | |
| **Total Scores** | - | | | |

**Figure C-17. Decision Matrix of Nonfunctional Requirements for the GreenBay Seafood Example**

# APPENDIX D. AN EXAMPLE OF OPEN SOURCE ERP SYSTEM *

## 1. Overview of ERP Systems

A large scale ERP system such as SAP, Oracle Applications, and The Sage Group is used for large business organizations. Microsoft Dynamics is suitable for medium-sized business organizations with up to about 2,250 users. It has rich functionality across financials, supply chain management, and customer relationship management. If a company is already using Microsoft Office and Windows, it would find that Microsoft Dynamics is easy to use and works smoothly with the familiar Microsoft products. Recently, open source ERP systems are widely available for medium or even small business organizations, such as webERP, Compiere, PostBooks, Opentaps, OpenERP, and OpenBravo.

An open source software product is free to use, and has a copyright license which allows end users to review and modify the source code for their own customization and/or troubleshooting needs. Open source licenses are also commonly free. One popular set of free open source software licenses are those approved by the Open Source Initiative (OSI) based on their Open Source Definition (OSD).

A business model behind an open source ERP system is the win-win relationship between the business community, the partner network, and the software editors. The partners are intended to create the market around the open source ERP system and to create services. The software editors are responsible for the quality and the vision on the development of the ERP system. The business community generates activities and contributes to the growth of the ERP system. All modules produced by the software editors, the partners and the community are to be open source. The user of an open source ERP system does not automatically receive system support

---

* **Acknowledgement:** The screenshots of webERP are reprinted from <www.weberp.org> with permission of Mr. Phil Daintree, the founder of webERP and one of the main contributors.

and services directly from anyone. However, an open source ERP system has its active social network that can create service offers and deals.

After reviewing dozen open source ERP systems, we found that webERP is one of the best open source ERP systems on the Internet. This appendix provides an introduction to webERP and samples of user interface of webERP for a variety of functionalities and configuring operations.

## 2. webERP

webERP (www.weberp.org) is a complete Web-based ERP system with emphasis on accounting. The open source ERP system requires only a Web-browser and PDF reader to use. It has a wide range of functions that support many business processes of wholesale, distribution, and manufacturing:

- Order entry
- Taxes
- Accounts payable
- Accounts receivable
- Inventory
- Purchasing
- Banking
- General ledger
- Production
- Contract costing
- Fixed assets

webERP can be easily configured on any operating system and the computer processing requirements are light. webERP can be run over an internal LAN. It can also be run on a third party web-hosting server external to the business which needs only a router and connection to the Internet to use webERP. It supports multiple languages for international users. webERP is a pioneer of "**cloud computing**" where the application can take place anywhere on the Internet and be delivered to the business through "the cloud".

Besides the official Web site of webERP, there are two main types of support of webERP.

1. Community Support - There are mailing lists that consist of all the developers and users of webERP. The webERP mailing lists can be accessed via the nabble forum (www.nabble.com), and are the best places to inquire about any issue you may have with using or developing webERP. The users archives and developer archives of the mailing lists contain valuable knowledge.

2. Commercial Support - Several companies offer commercial support which may be preferable for ordinary business organizations.

## 3. Sample of user interface of webERP

**Sales dashboard** – It lists orders, quotations, and summaries of sales orders, invoices, prices, and other report links.

**Receivables dashboard** – It links to receipts, invoices, statements, overdue records, daily transactions, and others.

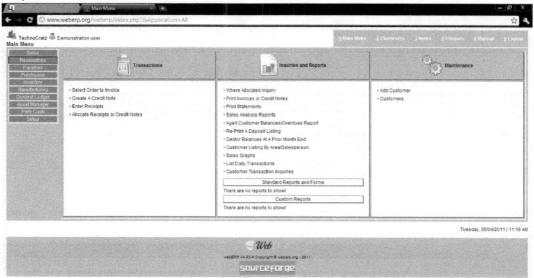

**Payables dashboard** - It contains vendor related links similar to receivables dashboard.

**Purchases dashboard** - It shows the status of various purchase orders and shipment entries.

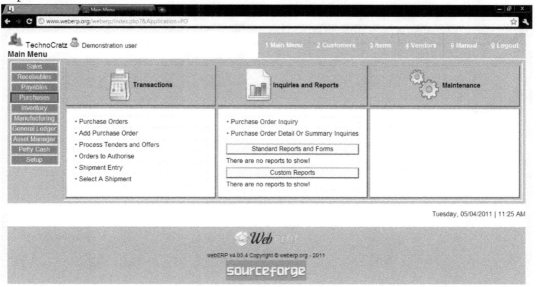

**Inventory dashboard** – It shows inventory related transactions and reports. It also allows the user to add, update, or delete inventory items.

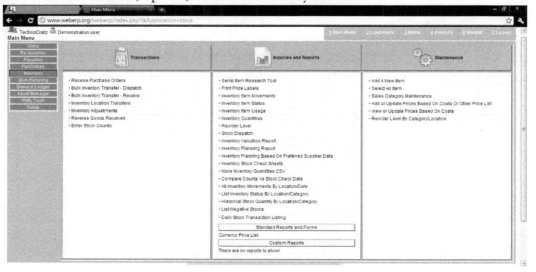

**Manufacturing dashboard** - It links to work order entry, materials inquiries, and other reports. It allows the user to perform MRP calculation.

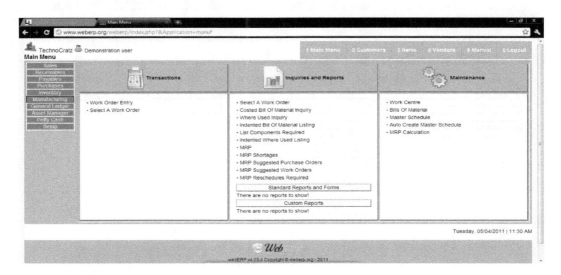

**General ledger dashboard** - It links to all entries of customer and supplier invoices, refunds, payment, bank statements, account inquiries, and others.

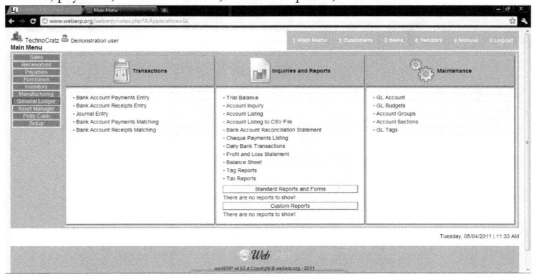

**Asset manager dashboard** - It has asset related links that allow the user to add or delete asset, change asset location, and other operations.

Before an ERP system can operate, configuring must be done to set many attributes or parameters (e.g., structures, terminology, access rights, etc.) of the system for the organization to meet the specific needs in the best possible way. webERP has a central dashboard for links of configuring functions. The following screenshots are examples of configuring webERP.

**Set up dashboard** – It links to configure operations for entire ERP settings.

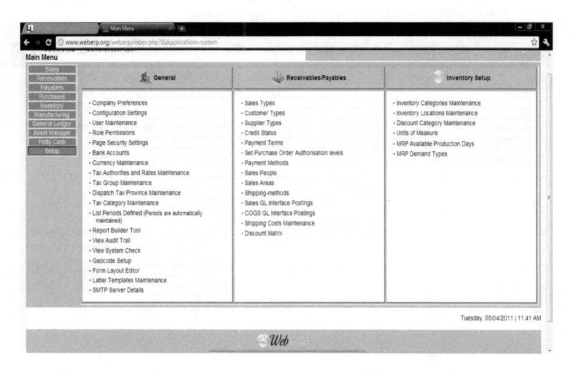

## Configuring webERP using Installation Wizard

**Welcome to the WebERP Installation Wizard.**

## Step 1

Please check the following requirements are met before continuing...

PHP Version > 4.1.0  **Yes**    PHP Session Support  **Enabled**    PHP Safe Mode  **Disabled**

## Step 2

Please check the following files/folders are writeable before continuing...

Configuration file  **Unwriteable**    Company data dirs (../companies/*)  **Unwriteable**

## Step 3

Please check your path settings...

Absolute URL:  `http://localhost/webERP/`

## Step 4

Please specify your operating system information below...

Server Operating System:    ◉ Linux/Unix based    ☐ World-writeable file permissions (777)
                            ○ Windows    (Please note: this is only recommended for testing environments)

Please enter your MySQL database server details below...

Host Name:  `localhost`    Username:  `root`

Password:  ●●

☑ Install Tables
(Please note: May remove existing tables and data)

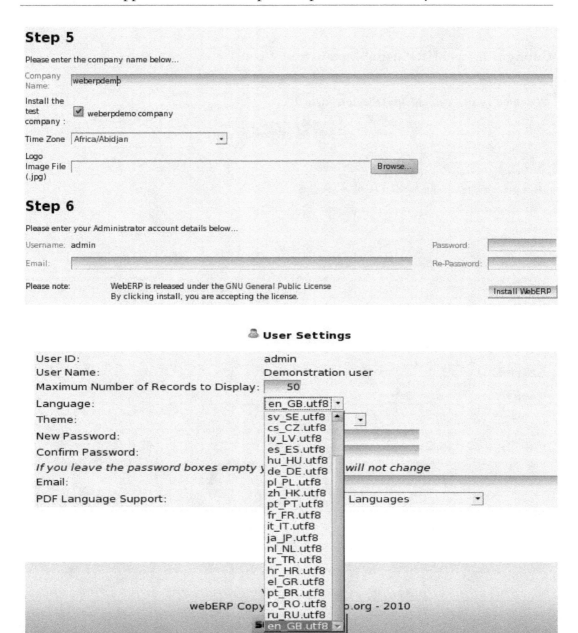

**Step 5**

Please enter the company name below...

Company Name: weberpdemp

Install the test company : ☑ weberpdemo company

Time Zone  Africa/Abidjan

Logo Image File (.jpg)  _____  Browse...

**Step 6**

Please enter your Administrator account details below...

Username: admin                                                    Password: _____

Email: _____                  Re-Password: _____

Please note:    WebERP is released under the GNU General Public License
                By clicking install, you are accepting the license.                    Install WebERP

---

🖳 **User Settings**

User ID:                                          admin
User Name:                                        Demonstration user
Maximum Number of Records to Display:             50
Language:                                         en_GB.utf8 ▾
Theme:                                            sv_SE.utf8 ▲    ▾
New Password:                                     cs_CZ.utf8
                                                  lv_LV.utf8
Confirm Password:                                 es_ES.utf8
                                                  hu_HU.utf8
*If you leave the password boxes empty* ⟩  de_DE.utf8  *will not change*
                                                  pl_PL.utf8
Email:                                            zh_HK.utf8
PDF Language Support:                             pt_PT.utf8    Languages          ▾
                                                  fr_FR.utf8
                                                  it_IT.utf8
                                                  ja_JP.utf8
                                                  nl_NL.utf8
                                                  tr_TR.utf8
                                                  hr_HR.utf8
                                                  el_GR.utf8
                                                  pt_BR.utf8
                        webERP Copy  ro_RO.utf8  o.org - 2010
                                     ru_RU.utf8
                                  S en_GB.utf8 ▾

# INDEX

## A

adaptive maintenance, 138

Adding supplemental software product, 113

adjusting system requirements, 114

agile development, 34

alpha testing, 131

alternatives, 104

analysis phase, 20

analytical hierarchy process (AHP), 109

Analyze (in Visible Analyst), 163

as-is system, 20, 38

## B

backward-design, 111

balancing, 76

basic physical structures, 102

beta testing, 131

break-even point method, 45

budgeting, 45

business function, 49

business operation, 49

business process, 49, 56, 95

business process automation (BPA), 39

business process improvement (BPI), 39

business process model, 56, 57, 97

business process modeling, 13, 56, 97, 150

Business Process Modeling Notation (BPMN), 59

business process modeling tool, 57

business process reengineering (BPR), 39, 40

business rule, 51

business scenario, 49

## C

CASE (Computer Aided Systems Engineering) tools, 23, 78, 149

CASE repository, 78, 149

cash flow method, 43

class, 63

cloud computing, 24, 116, 190

Color (in Visible Analyst), 169

conducting interview, 54

configuring, 128, 195

consistency, 123

constraints, 40

context diagram, 69

contingency plan, 133

corrective maintenance, 137

cost-benefit analysis, 42

customizing, 113, 128

## D

data, 50

# POWERPOINT SLIDES

S1

## Information Systems
## Analysis and Design

Shouhong Wang, PhD

*Charlton College of Business*
*University of Massachusetts Dartmouth*

Copyright Shouhong Wang 2011

---

S2

**PREFACE**
*(Major Coverage of the book)*

- **Theme of Information Systems Analysis and Design**
- The right process of information systems development for the organization.
- Tools that can be applied to the information systems development.

© Copyright Shouhong Wang 2011

---

S3

PREFACE (cont'd)

- This course focuses on business process modeling
- It discusses data modeling, networking, computer programming, and computer hardware and operating systems very briefly in delivering the monolithic concept of information systems development.

Copyright Shouhong Wang 2011

---

S4

PREFACE (cont'd)

**Unique features of this textbook**

- *Emphasizing information systems acquisition instead of systems construction.*
- *Emphasizing the systems acquisition tools instead of the system construction tools.*
- *Emphasizing contemporary contents instead of legacy contents*
- *Emphasizing project skills*
- *Eliminating secondary material*

Copyright Shouhong Wang 2011

---

S5

PREFACE (cont'd)

**The organization of this textbook**

- Chapter 1: Introduction.
- Chapter 2: Information systems development approaches.
- Chapter 3: Systems planning.
- Chapter 4: Systems analysis.
- Chapter 5: Systems design.
- Chapter 6: Systems implementation.
- Chapter 7: Systems maintenance.
- Appendix A: Guideline for course projects .
- Appendix B: Tutorial of CASE tool: Visible Analysis.
- Appendix C: A Project Example
- Appendix D: Open Source ERP Systems

Copyright Shouhong Wang 2011

S1

**CHAPTER 1.
INTRODUCTION**

Copyright Shouhong Wang 2011

S4

**1.2. Central Objective of Information Systems Development**

- The central objective of information systems development is to create **value** for the organization by using information technology.
- For most business firms, value means more profits. For non-for-profit organizations and government agencies, value can mean much more than monetary measures.

Copyright Shouhong Wang 2011

S2

**1.1. Context of Information Systems Analysis and Design**

- An **information system** is an organized collection of people, information technology, information resources, and all coordinated activities to achieve certain objectives in the business organization.
- **Information systems development** covers a wide range of technical areas including business process modeling, data modeling and database design, networking design, computer programming, and computer hardware and operating systems.

Copyright Shouhong Wang 2011

S5

**1.2. Central Objective of Information Systems Development (cont'd)**

- **Success factors** for information systems development:

- Top management support;
- User involvement;
- Alignment of the business strategy and the project strategy;
- Effective project management;
- Organizational collaboration; etc.

Copyright Shouhong Wang 2011

S3

**1.1. Context of Information Systems Analysis and Design (cont'd)**

- **Information systems analysis and design** is the process of completing an information systems development project.

Copyright Shouhong Wang 2011

S6

**1.3. Systems Analysts**

- Business skills
- Information technology skills
- Human interaction skills
- Managerial skills

Copyright Shouhong Wang 2011

S1

# CHAPTER 2.
# INFORMATION SYSTEMS
# DEVELOPMENT

Copyright Shouhong Wang 2011

S4

**2.1. Systems Development Life Cycle (cont'd)**

- (1) The system development process of an information system must move through these five phases.

- (2) Each of the five phases produces a set of reports, called deliverable, which is used as input for the its successor phase.

Copyright Shouhong Wang 2011

S2

**2.1. Systems Development Life Cycle**

- The **Systems development life cycle** (**SDLC**) is the general conceptual model of the phases an information system goes through.

Copyright Shouhong Wang 2011

S5

**2.1. Systems Development Life Cycle (cont'd)**

- The **planning phase** is the process of preliminary investigation to understand **why** a new information system should be created for the organization.

- The deliverable of the planning phase includes a report of the feasibility study and a workplan for the new information system development.

Copyright Shouhong Wang 2011

S3

**2.1. Systems Development Life Cycle (cont'd)**

**Systems development life cycle (SDLC)**

Copyright Shouhong Wang 2011

S6

**2.1. Systems Development Life Cycle (cont'd)**

- The **analysis phase** is to investigate **what** the new information system will do.
- In this phase, the project team fully investigates the current information system (or the **as-is** system).
- The specific business needs (or the **system requirements)** for the new information system.
- The new information system that meets the system requirements is called the **to-be** system.

Copyright Shouhong Wang 2011

207

S7

### 2.1. Systems Development Life Cycle (cont'd)

- The deliverable of the analysis phase reports on the following major analysis results:

- The differences between the as-is system and to-be system;
- the system requirements for the to-be system;
- the strategy of the system development for the design phase.

Copyright Shouhong Wang 2011

S10

### 2.1. Systems Development Life Cycle (cont'd)

- The **maintenance phase** improves the new information system.
- Because of the innovation of IT and significant changes in the business environment, the cost of system maintenance eventually becomes unjustified at a certain point.
- The information system development starts a new cycle.

Copyright Shouhong Wang 2011

S8

### 2.1. Systems Development Life Cycle (cont'd)

- The **design phase** determines *how* the to-be system is created and will operate in terms of hardware, software, networking, system personnel, and operational procedures.
- The deliverables of the design phase are the detailed specifications of hardware, software, and networking for the to-be system.
- The design phase actually provides the solution to the to-be system.

Copyright Shouhong Wang 2011

S11

### 2.2. Management of Systems Development Project

**2.2.1. Project sponsor and project approval**
- An information system project in the organization must have its **project sponsor** who holds a top position in the organization (e.g., VP).
- An information system project must be approved by the organization. Approval procedures might vary depending upon the organizational structures.

Copyright Shouhong Wang 2011

S9

### 2.1. Systems Development Life Cycle (cont'd)

- The **implementation phase** builds the new information system based on the specifications of the system provided by the design phase
- By the end of the implementation phase, the new information system replaces the old information system.

Copyright Shouhong Wang 2011

S12

### 2.2. Management of Systems Development Project (cont'd)

**2.2.2. Project scope definition, project scale estimation, and risk assessment**
- The **project scope** defines the range of system requirements of the organization for the new information system.
- **Scope creep** : new components are added to the project after the scope has been defined.
- **Project scale**: budget, time duration, and manpower.
- **Risk** of failure – risk assessment

Copyright Shouhong Wang 2011

**S13**

## 2.2. Management of Systems Development Project (cont'd)

### 2.2.3. Project team management

- The project team is crucial for the success of the project.
- Rewarding methods to motivate the information systems professionals, such as recognition, advancement, and self-regulation.
- Promote knowledge sharing and collaboration through the use of **CASE (Computer Aided Systems Engineering)** tools and Web2.0 techniques.

**S14**

## 2.2. Management of Systems Development Project (cont'd)

### 2.2.4. Project control and coordination

- Project management software packages (e.g., Microsoft Project) for the information systems project control and coordination
- Compiling the workplan of project.
- Generating the Gantt chart or PERT chart for time management.
- However, CASE tools must be used for information system projects
  (e.g., ensuring the **system standards**).

**S15**

## 2.3. Fundamental Strategies of Information Systems Development in Organizations

- **Information systems development strategy** is a plan of action designed to allow the organization to concentrate its limited resources on the greatest opportunities of information system development.
- Three fundamental information systems development strategies: systems acquisition, systems construction, and outsourcing.

**S16**

## 2.3. Fundamental Strategies of Information Systems Development in Organizations: Trends

**S17**

## 2.3.1. Systems acquisition

- **Systems acquisition**: to use commercialized business applications software products on the market for the new information system.
- **Off-the-shelf software packages** for small middle-size business organizations.
- **ERP systems** are used for large business organizations.
- **SaaS** (Software as a Service) for very typical business processes through the Internet (*cloud computing technology*).

**S18**

## 2.3.1. Systems acquisition (cont'd)

Information Systems Acquisition

S19

### 2.3.2. Systems construction

- **Systems construction**: construct an information system in-house by using computer programming tools and database management systems.
- It was popular decades ago.
- Now, only cutting-edge IT companies do this.

Copyright Shouhong Wang 2011

S22

### Comparison of development strategies

| Fundamental Systems Development Strategies | | System Scale | System Uniqueness | Development Time Duration | Development Costs | System Test and Quality Assurance | Project Control of the organization |
|---|---|---|---|---|---|---|---|
| | | | | Systems Development Characteristics | | | |
| Systems Acquisition | Off-the-Shelf Package | Small to middle | Generic with little variation | Quick | Very Low | Producer or vendors | Simple |
| | ERP Systems | Middle to large | Generic with configuration and customization features | Short | Low | Producer or vendors | Vendor is usually involved |
| | SaaS | Simple application | Generic | Instant | Extremely Low | Service provider | Very simple |
| Systems Construction | | Vary | Unique | Long | High | Uncertain until the system runs for a time period | Complicated |
| Outsourcing | | Vary depending on the contract | Vary depending on the contract | Vary depending on the contract | Vary depending on the contract | Vary depending on contract | Low control |

Copyright Shouhong Wang 2011

S20

### 2.3.2. Systems construction (cont'd)

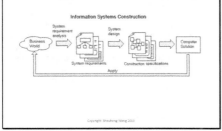

Copyright Shouhong Wang 2011

S23

### 2.4. Diversified Information System Construction Approaches

- **Waterfall approach:** The traditional approach to constructing a new system that follows the classical SDLC model

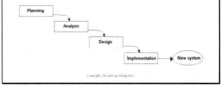

Copyright Shouhong Wang 2011

S21

### 2.3.3. Outsourcing

- Outsourcing: contracting out of the systems development jobs to an external service provider(s).
- **Request for Proposal (RFP)** to search the best service provider for the systems development project.
- A project liaison cooperates with the outsourcing firm and monitors the progress of the outsourced project.

Copyright Shouhong Wang 2011

S24

### 2.4.1. Waterfall approach

- Advantage: each phase of the development process produces clear and detailed documentations for the next phase.
- Disadvantage: the development process takes a long time to deliver the final new information system.
- For the large systems with clear and stable system requirements.

Copyright Shouhong Wang 2011

S25

### 2.4.2. Parallel approach

- **Parallel approach** divides the system construction project into several subprojects that can be analyzed, designed, and implemented in parallel.

Copyright Shouhong Wang 2011

S28

### 2.4.3. Rapid application development (RAD) approach: Prototyping (cont'd)

- A **system prototype** is a model product that represents main features of the target system, but is not an operational system.

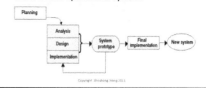

Copyright Shouhong Wang 2011

S26

### 2.4.2. Parallel approach (cont'd)

- Advantage: the project duration can be reduced significantly in comparison with the waterfall approach.
- Disadvantage : the subprojects are usually not independent and the complicated interrelationships between the subprojects often cause difficulties for the system integration.

Copyright Shouhong Wang 2011

S29

### 2.4.4. Other variant approaches of RAP

- **Extreme Programming (XP)** is a lightweight system construction approach. The construction team is small (e.g., 2 to 12 people). Coding is always performed by pairs of programmers. The team keeps close interaction with the users.
- **Agile development** is a generalization of XP, but does not require pair programming.
- The **reuse-based development** approach emphasizes software reuse.

Copyright Shouhong Wang 2011

S27

### 2.4.3. Rapid application development (RAD) approach

- **Rapid application development (RAD)**: a type of systems construction that uses minimal planning, analysis, and design in favor of rapid construction prototyping.
- Using the RAD approach, the planning, analysis, and design activities are interleaved with writing the software itself, and the documentations of planning, analysis, and design are reduced to virtually none.

Copyright Shouhong Wang 2011

**S1**

# CHAPTER 3.
# SYSTEMS PLANNING

Copyright Shouhong Wang 2011

**S4**

### 3.1. Initiating a System Development Project (cont'd)

- **System request** describes the considerations and the rationale of a new information system development project, and the development strategy (i.e., systems acquisition, or systems construction), to the organization for approval.
- The approval procedure follows the organizational policy and rules.

Copyright Shouhong Wang 2011

**S2**

## CHAPTER 3. SYSTEMS PLANNING

- The **systems planning phase** is the process of preliminary investigation to understand why a new information system should be created for the organization. It includes the following major steps.
- (1) Initiating a system development project.
- (2) Defining the scope of the target system development project.
- (3) Justifying of the feasibility.
- (4) Scheduling the tasks.
- (5) Assessing risks.
- (6) Generating a system development project plan.

Copyright Shouhong Wang 2011

**S5**

### 3.1. Initiating a System Development Project (cont'd)

- **Feasibility study**: a preliminary systems analysis without great details. for the system development project.
- A feasibility study includes three steps:
- Defining the scope of the new information system
- Justifying the feasibility
- Generating a system development project plan

Copyright Shouhong Wang 2011

**S3**

### 3.1. Initiating a System Development Project

- New business needs could occur when
- (1) the organization recognizes its problems of information processing;
- (2) the organization explores new opportunities of information technology;
- (3) the organization makes a proactive action in response to the business environment changes.

Copyright Shouhong Wang 2011

**S6**

### 3.2. Defining the Scope of the Target New Information System

#### 3.2.1. As-Is system

- (1) What stakeholders of the organization will be affected by the system development project, and how each of these stakeholders uses the current information system.
- (2) What business processes will be affected by the development project, and what the current form of each of these business processes is.
- (3) What organizational units will be affected the system development project, and how each of these organizational units plays a part of the current information system.

Copyright Shouhong Wang 2011

S7

**3.2. Defining the Scope of the Target New Information System (cont'd)**

**3.2.2. To-Be system**

- (1) How each of the affected stakeholders uses the new information system.
- (2) What the form of each of the affected business processes will be.
- (3) How each of the affected organizational units plays a part of the new information system.

S10

**Business Process Improvement (BPI)**

- **BPI** is to improve business processes. The objective of a BPI project is to improve the organizational business process effectiveness in addition to the efficiency.
- There is a change to the current organizational business process.
- Because of the potential changes of the organizational business process, the risk of failure in a BPI project could be higher in comparison with a BPA project.

S8

**3.2.3. Extent of the potential changes of the business process**

- The extent of the potential changes of the business process can be categorized into
- Business process automation (BPA)
- Business process improvement (BPI)
- Business process reengineering (BPR)

S11

**Business Process Reengineering (BPR)**

- **BPR** is to make radical changes to the current organizational business process.
- The organizational business process will be changed radically. The current as-is system is not worth examination in detail. Extensive investigation of the to-be system is needed.
- Because of the radical changes of the organizational business process, the risk of failure in a BPR project is usually high.

S9

**Business Process Automation (BPA)**

- **BPA** is to automate manual processes by using computerized information systems.
- The process logics of the as-is system and the to-be system are similar except for that the to-be system is computerized. Thus, the changes to the organizational business process are minor.
- The risk of failure in a BPA project is low.
- The limitation of BPA is that the advantages of computerized information systems is underexplored.

S12

**3.3. Justifying the Feasibility**

- Constraints
- Technological feasibility
- Economic feasibility
- Organizational feasibility.

S13

### 3.3.1. Constraints

- Limited financial resources (budget);
- Imperfect human resources competency of the organization;
- Inadequate computing support facilities;
- The current platform of information system;
- Insufficient physical facilities;
- Possible conflicts caused by the project; and
- Unresolved legal issues related to the new information system.

S16

### Costs

- Tangible costs: easy to measure
- Intangible costs: difficult to measure

- Tangible Costs:
- **Development costs** (for creating the system)
- **Operational costs** (for day-to-day operations)

S14

### 3.3.2. Technological feasibility

- "Is the technology ready for this project?"

- The information system development strategy:
  Acquisition or construction?

- System compatibility

S17

### Benefits

- Tangible benefits: easy to measure
- Intangible benefits: difficult to measure

- Tangible benefits:
  Manpower saving, increasing sales ....

- Intangible benefits:
  Long-term strategies ....

S15

### 3.3.3. Economic feasibility

- *"Can we afford the project?"*

- **Cost-benefit analysis** is to determine the benefits and savings that are expected from the new information system and to compare them with the costs.

S18

### Cost-benefit analysis techniques

- **Cash flow method** - net present values
- **Return on investment method** - The return on investment (ROI)
- **Break-even point method**

S19

S22

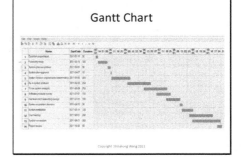

S20

### *3.3.4. Organizational feasibility*

- *"Would people like the new system?"*
- Stakeholders of the organization
- Stockholders of the organization
- Managers at all levels
- Users of the system.

S23

### 3.5. Assessing Risks

- Overly optimistic schedule;
- Underestimated budget;
- High turnover rate of project team members;
- Unstable vendors; and
- Volatile business environment.

S21

### 3.4. Scheduling the Project Activities

- **Activities of the project.**
- Attributes of an activity:
- name of the activity;
- definition of the activity;
- duration of the activity;
- prerequisite activity of the activity;
- starting time and finishing time of the activity;
- responsible personnel of the activity.

S24

### 3.6. Generating a System Development Project Plan

- **Project plan**

- Scope of the project.
- Feasibility study results.
- Schedule of project activities.
- Risk assessment.
- Budget and other resource needs.

S25

### Your Project

- 1. Meet your group members to identify a business organization which is going to use information technology to improve its business processes. Small business is ideal. A department of a middle-size organization is also feasible. One or more group members must be familiar with the business firm so that the systems requirement analysis would not heavily rely on interviews.
- 2. Verbally discuss the scope of your project in terms of the business process you are going to investigate.

S26

### Your Project (cont'd)

- 3. Identify the problems of the current business process, and opportunities of improvement.
- 4. Verbally describe the as-is system of the organization.
- 5. Verbally discuss your vision of the to-be system for the organization. Identify the components of BPA and BPI for the business process.
- 6. Discuss the feasibilities for the organization to implement the to-be system.
- 7. Discuss the constraints of the organization for the to-be system.

**S1**

## CHAPTER 4.
## SYSTEMS ANALYSIS

Copyright Shouhong Wang 2011

**S2**

### CHAPTER 4. SYSTEMS ANALYSIS

- **The systems analysis phase** is to determine the requirements for the new information system.
- (1) Collecting information for understanding the system requirements.
- (2) Specifying the system requirements using modeling techniques.
- (3) Contrasting the as-is system and the to-be system in terms of system requirements.
- (4) Documenting the system requirements for the systems design phase.

Copyright Shouhong Wang 2011

**S3**

### 4.1. System Requirements

- A **system requirement** is a statement or expression that specifies what the information system must perform or what characteristics the information system must have.
- Functional requirements
- Nonfunctional requirements

Copyright Shouhong Wang 2011

**S4**

### 4.1.1. Functional requirements

- A **functional requirement** specifies what the information system must do to accomplish the business processes, the information provision, and the business rules of the organization.

Copyright Shouhong Wang 2011

**S5**

### (1) Business process

- A business process is a set of business activities performed by human actors and/or the information system to accomplish a specific outcome.

Copyright Shouhong Wang 2011

**S6**

### (2) User-perceived information

- **A piece of user-perceived information is always associated with a process.**
- **Input** is the acquired information captured by the process.
- **Output** is the delivered information produced by the business process.
- **Navigation information** provides the direction for the user to proceed through the business process.

Copyright Shouhong Wang 2011

S7

### (3) **Business rules**

- A **business rule** is a statement that aims to influence or guide business processes in the organization.
- A business rule specifies the relationships between an anticipated condition and expected actions or outcomes.

Copyright Shouhong Wong 2011

S10

### (2) **Security**

- The system should have safeguards against unauthorized access, cyber attacks, and information loss.

Copyright Shouhong Wong 2011

S8

### 4.1.2. Nonfunctional requirements

- A **nonfunctional requirement** specifies a characteristic or property of the information system must have.

Copyright Shouhong Wong 2011

S11

### (3) **Vendor**

- Reputation.
- Services such as maintenance and upgrading.
- Business alliance for the long term consideration.
- Training availability.
- Standardization and industrial common platform.

Copyright Shouhong Wong 2011

S9

### (1) **Usability requirements**

- **Usability** requirements specify the user-friendliness of the information system.
- Quality of the user interface of the system, and the easiness of use.
- Degree of error tolerance.
- Quality of documentation, including **reference documents**, **operation manuals**, and **tutorials**.
- Unique operational features, e.g., data visualization.

Copyright Shouhong Wong 2011

S12

### (4) **Performance**

- Reliability - the extent to which the system is available to the users in all circumstances.
- **Scalability** - the ability of the system to increase the capacity in response to additional needs.
- Speed - the time for the business processes.

Copyright Shouhong Wong 2011

S13

### (5) Others

- Multiple languages.
- Pricing competitiveness.
- Cultural and religion consideration.

S16

### 4.2.3. Joint Analytical Development (JAD)

- **Joint Analytical Development (JAD)** is a team-based requirements information collection technique.
- The objective of JAD is to bring representatives of all stakeholders of the organization together to identify system requirements

S14

### 4.2. Techniques of Requirements Information Collection

#### *4.2.1. Experiencing and observation*

- It is ideal for the systems analysts to have **first-hand experiences** of the pertinent business processes as the user of the information system in that organization.
- **Observation** is the act of watching ongoing business processes.

S17

### 4.2.4. Documents review

- A **documents review** is to analyze the documentation of the as-is system, including the previous systems analysis and design reports for the as-is system as well as operational and maintenance records, to understand the requirements for the to-be system.

S15

### *4.2.2. Interview*

- **Interview** is the most commonly used technique for requirements information collecting. It can reach a wide range of the users of the information system including managers, operational staff, and customers.
- (1) **Designing interview questions**
- (2) **Selecting interviewees**
- (3) **Conducting interview**
- (4) **Verifying and releasing interview findings**

S18

### 4.2.5. Questionnaire

- A **questionnaire** is a survey instrument that consists of a series of written questions for collecting information from respondents.
- The responses rates of questionnaires are usually low.

**S19**

### 4.2.6. Selecting techniques for collecting requirements information

- The systems analysts must select several techniques, given the fact that none of these techniques is perfect for systems analysis.
- Select best techniques to ensure that all functional requirements and nonfunctional requirements for the to-be system are complete, unbiased, and accurate.

Copyright Shouhong Wang 2011

**S22**

### 4.3. Business Process Modeling (cont'd)

- A **business process model** is a model that defines the way in which business activities are carried out to accomplish the intended goal of the entire business process.
- A business process model describes the business processes and the integration of these processes at multiple abstraction levels.

Copyright Shouhong Wang 2011

**S20**

### 4.3. Business Process Modeling

- **Business process modeling** is the primary systems modeling work for systems analysis and design because the **business process model** of the organization is the central abstraction that describes the business functional requirements and lays the foundation for other system models in the system development.

Copyright Shouhong Wang 2011

**S23**

### 4.4. Major Tools of Business Process Modeling

- A **business process modeling tool** is a **formalized visual language** that provides systems analysts with the ability to describe the business processes unambiguously, to visualize the business processes for systematic understanding, and to communicate the business process models for the information systems development.

Copyright Shouhong Wang 2011

**S21**

### 4.3. Business Process Modeling (cont'd)

- A **business process** is a collection of related and structured activities or tasks that produce a specific output(s) in response to an input (s).
- (1) A **management process** is a managerial decision making process.
- (2) An **operational process** is a business process of routine business operations.
- (3) A **supporting process** is a business process that supports management processes and operational processes.

Copyright Shouhong Wang 2011

**S24**

### 4.4.1. Data Flow Diagram (DFD)

- A **data flow diagram** (DFD) is a graphical representation of the business processes and the flows of data through an information system.
- The central concept of DFD is the **top-down approach** to understanding a system.
- The DFD tool is good at modeling business processes in the aspects of operation and data, but is weak in the aspect of business rules

Copyright Shouhong Wang 2011

S25

### 4.4.1. DFD (cont'd)

- A business process can be **decomposed** into several sub-processes.
- Each of the sub-processes has its own goal of transforming its input into the output, and can be further decomposed into its sub-processes.

S28

### 4.4.3. Business Process Modeling Notations (BPMN)

- BPMN is a graphical representation for specifying sequences and steps of business processes.
- BPMN can provide detailed specifications for automation of business processes, and thus are ideal for systems construction, but is short of the ability of top-down system modeling.

S26

### 4.4.2. Unified Modeling Language (UML)

- The UML is a general-purpose modeling tool in the field of software engineering for constructing all types of computerized systems including computer operating systems, industrial control systems, geographical information systems, image processing systems, data communication systems, business information systems, and others.
- The object-oriented approach views a system as a collection of self-contained objects, including both data and processes.

S29

### 4.4.4. Summary of business process modeling tools

- The business process modeling tool used for systems acquisition development must be effective for examinations of software products.
- DFD is a practically workable tool for systems acquisition development in comparison with other builder-centered business process modeling tools.

S27

### 4.4.2. UML (cont'd)

- The UML includes a set of various types of diagrams with different subjects of modeling and diversified graphics styles.
- Four dominant UML diagramming techniques are: use case diagrams, class diagrams, sequence diagrams, and behavior state machine diagrams.
- It is good for software construction, but is weak in business process modeling.

S30

### 4.5. Data Flow Diagram

**4.5.1. Overview of DFD**

**S31**

- Client sends inquiries, advertising job orders, and requests for changes to the job orders to the advertising firm.
- The client service makes several actions (or processes) in response to the client's inputs.
- The cline service also files advertising job order for the client, and sends the order to another process called "Job Scheduling".
- The client service has the responsibility to inform the client once the advertising job order has been scheduled.
- Two data stores are used for the client service: "Client Data" and "Job Schedules".
- There are many data flows in the client service.

Copyright: Shouhong Wang 2011

**S32**

## Important properties of DFD

- DFD is a better tool than natural languages (e.g., English).
- DFD is quite simple to use, and is easy to understand.
- The processes expressed in a DFD may or may not operate sequentially..
- This example of DFD represents a simple business process. If the business process is complicated, a one-page DFD can be huge. A huge DFD is not practically usable for communicating system requirements.

Copyright: Shouhong Wang 2011

**S33**

### DFD Elements

| DFD Elements | Symbols | Explanations |
|---|---|---|
| External Entity | Name | An external entity is a class of persons or a class of organizations outside the system. It provides the source of data for the system and/or receives the data from the system. The name of an external entity is a unique noun. |
| Process | ID Name | A process is set of business activities of the system. It processes the input and produces the output. The name of a process is a unique verb or verb phrase. Each process has its unique identification number (ID). The value of ID is not important, but indicates the level of the process. |
| Data Store | ID Name | A data store is a data repository of a set of integrated data used by the system. It can be a data file, a data table, or a set of data tables. A data store has a unique noun, and a unique identification number (ID). The value of ID is not important. |
| Data Flow | Name | A data flow is an instance of data item or a set of data that flows between an external entity and process, or between two processes, or between a process and a data store. The name of a data flow is a unique noun. |

Copyright: Shouhong Wang 2011

**S34**

### 4.5.2. Systems thinking approach

- A **system** is a set of interacting or interdependent components that form an integrated whole to achieve a certain goal.

- An information system is a system.

Copyright: Shouhong Wang 2011

**S35**

### 4.5.2. Systems thinking approach (cont'd)

- **Systems thinking** is the process of understanding how components of the system influence one another within a whole.
- Systems thinking provides a view of the business process as a whole in the context of information services, and concerns an understanding of the linkages and interactions between the elements that compose the entirety of the information system.

Copyright: Shouhong Wang 2011

**S36**

### 4.5.2. Systems thinking approach (cont'd)

**Systems Thinking: Information System Entirety**

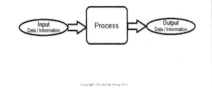

Copyright: Shouhong Wang 2011

222

S37

### 4.5.2. Systems thinking approach (cont'd)

**Systems Thinking Approach to Information Systems Analysis: Top-down Decomposition**

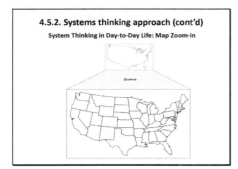

S40

### 4.5.3. Context diagram (cont'd)

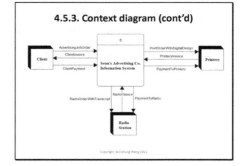

S38

### 4.5.2. Systems thinking approach (cont'd)

**System Thinking in Day-to-Day Life: Map Zoom-in**

S41

### 4.5.3. Context diagram (cont'd)

- A context diagram has the following characteristics.
- (1) A context diagram has a single overall process that represents the entire information system.
- (2) A context diagram includes all external entities.
- (3) A context diagram includes all major data flows that represent the substantial interactions with the external entities.
- (4) A context diagram does not show data stores which are inside the overall process.

S39

### 4.5.3. Context diagram

- A **context diagram** shows the entire system as a single process, and represents the system's interactions with the environment using data flows.
- A context diagram is also commonly known as "**Level-0 DFD**".

S42

### 4.5.4. Decomposition

- A context diagram describes the overall system, but does not describe perceptible and measureable system requirement in detail.
- To understand more about the information system, the system analysts must decompose the entire information system into **sub-systems**.
- To do so, **segments** are identified.

223

S43

### 4.5.4. Decomposition (cont'd)

- An **operational process** is a business process of routine business operations.
- A **management process** is a managerial decision making process, such as budgeting and supplier selection.
- A **supporting process** is a business process that supports management processes and operational processes.
- **Heuristics** are applied to identify segments for the system decomposition.

S44

### 4.5.4. Decomposition (cont'd)

(1) **Start with the external entities.**

*Heuristic-1: For each external entity, there is a segment which contains operation process and/or support process to provide information services to the external entity.*

S45

### 4.5.4. Decomposition (cont'd)

- For Client

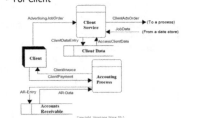

S46

### 4.5.4. Decomposition (cont'd)

- For Radio Station

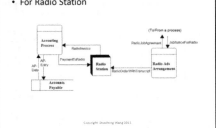

S47

### 4.5.4. Decomposition (cont'd)

- For Printery

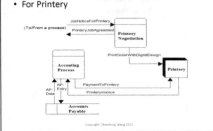

S48

### 4.5.4. Decomposition (cont'd)

- (2) **Move to organizational support.**

- *Heuristic-2: For each organizational function areas, including accounting, human resource management, marketing, finance, inventory management, and supplier chain management, identify a segment(s) with a general supporting process(es) that supports the processes in the identified segments for external entities.*

S49

### 4.5.4. Decomposition (cont'd)

- For Accounting Process

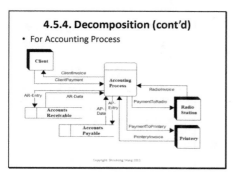

Copyright: Shouhong Wang 2011

S50

### 4.5.4. Decomposition (cont'd)

(3) **Move to managerial decisions.**

*Heuristic-3:* *Look into managerial decision processes that are applicable to the systems.*

Copyright: Shouhong Wang 2011

S51

### 4.5.4. Decomposition (cont'd)

- For Scheduling

Copyright: Shouhong Wang 2011

S52

### 4.5.4. Decomposition (cont'd)

- (1) System decomposition needs business skills and system thinking skills.
- (2) The decomposition procedure is rather artistic.
- (3) To describe the segments clearly, one step of decomposition creates around 7 (plus or minus 2) segments in common practices.
- (4) The identified segments should have overlaps with each other. This would make the integration of segments easier.

Copyright: Shouhong Wang 2011

S53

### 4.5.5. Level-1 diagram

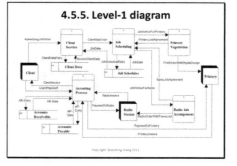

Copyright: Shouhong Wang 2011

S54

### 4.5.5. Level-1 diagram (cont'd)

- Each process, data store, data flow, and external entity has a unique name.
- Assign IDs to the processes and the data stores. The values of the IDs are not important.

Copyright: Shouhong Wang 2011

S55

## 4.5.5. Level-1 diagram (cont'd)

- The layout of DFD is not crucial.
- However, the number of data flows that cross each other should be minimized to avoid confusion or disorganization.
- Commonly, the shared data stores are placed in the middle of the diagram, the external entities are placed near the edges, and the processes are placed close to the data stores. If necessary, data stores and external entities can be duplicated.

S58

## 4.5.6. Balancing (cont'd)

**Simple rules can be applied to system decomposition:**

- Any external entity in the parent DFD must be kept in the children DFDs.
- Any data flow in the parent DFD must be kept in the children DFDs. In some cases, a data flow in the parent DFD can be split into two or more data flows in the children DFDs, but the data items conveyed by the data flow must not be lost.

S56

## 4.5.5. Level-1 diagram (cont'd)

- Generally, the processes represented in a Level-1 DFD operate in a parallel manner, and a sequential order between the processes may or may not exist.

S59

## 4.5.6. Balancing (cont'd)

**Simple rules can be applied to system decomposition (cont'd):**

- Any data store in the parent DFD must be kept in the children DFDs. In some cases, a data store in the parent DFD can be split into two or more data stores in the children DFDs, but the data items stored by the data store in the parent DFD must not be lost.

S57

## 4.5.6. Balancing

- Balancing refers to ensuring that the information presented in the parent DFD is accurately represented in its children DFDs.
- This does not mean that the information presented in the two generation DFD is identical.
- Balancing means that the children DFDs can always present more detailed information than the parent DFD does, but must not lose the information presented in the parent DFD.

S60

## 4.5.7. CASE tools

- CASE (Computer Aided Systems Engineering or Computer Aided Software Engineering) tools are a category of software that supports the information systems development process.

- The central component of a CASE tool is the **CASE repository** that stores all the diagrams and project information, and is shared by all project team members.

S61

### 4.5.7. CASE tools (cont'd)

- A CASE tool can be used to coordinate the project team activities, and to facilitate knowledge sharing among the project team members.
- A CASE tool allows the project team to follow the standard terminology.
- A CASE tool is not just a computer drawing tool. It can have intelligent features to verify the systems analysis and design results.
- A CASE tool can generate consistent documents with detailed information for each phase of the SDLC.

Copyright Shouhong Wang 2011

S62

### 4.5.8. Level-2 diagram

- Each process in the Level-1 DFD can be decomposed into a more detailed DFD, called a Level-2 DFD, in the similar way that the context diagram is decomposed into the Level-1 DFD.

Copyright Shouhong Wang 2011

S63

### 4.5.8. Level-2 diagram (cont'd)

**Client Service (Process-1) in Level-1 DFD is to be Decomposed**

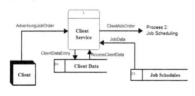

Copyright Shouhong Wang 2011

S64

### 4.5.8. Level-2 diagram (cont'd)

**Level-2 DFD of Decomposed Client Service (Process-1)**

Copyright Shouhong Wang 2011

S65

### 4.5.8. Level-2 diagram (cont'd)

- (1) Select a process in the Level-1 DFD to decompose it into the Level-2 DFD.
- (2) Include all external entities and data stores which are directly linked to the decomposed process in the Level-1 DFD (see the external entities and data stores marked in bold-line in Figure 4.14) in the Level-2 DFD (see the external entities and data stores marked in bold-line in Figure 4.15).
- (3) Include all data flows in the Level-1 DFD which are directly attached to the decomposed process (see the data flows marked in bold-line in Figure 4.14) in the Level-2 DFD (see the data flows marked in bold-line in Figure 4.15).

Copyright Shouhong Wang 2011

S66

### 4.5.8. Level-2 diagram (cont'd)

- (4) Replace the decomposed process in the Level-1 DFD with several (e.g., 7 plus and minus 2) detailed processes for the Level-2 DFD, and link all external entities, data flows, and data stores inherited from the Level-1 DFD to the processes in the Level-2 DFD (see the part marked in bold-line in Figure 4.15).
- (5) Create data flows between the detailed processes in the Level-2 DFD. New secondary data flows to or from the external entities as well as new detailed data stores may be added if needed (see the data flows to/from Client in fine-line in Figure 4.15).

Copyright Shouhong Wang 2011

S67

### 4.5.8. Level-2 diagram (cont'd)

- (6) Assign an ID for each detailed process in the Level-2 DFD, following the DFD convention that a process ID in the Level-2 DFD is an extension of the process ID of its parent (Level-1) process. For example, the process ID in the Level-1 DFD is "1", and the its children processes' IDs in the Level-2 DFD would be "1.1", "1.2", and so on (see Figure 4.15).

S70

### 4.5.9. Scope of system and lower level DFD (cont'd)

- **Primitive processes**: a process can be described clearly in no more than a dozen lines of short sentences of English, so-called **structured English**.

S68

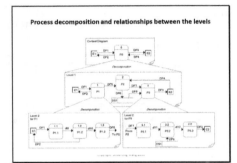

S71

### 4.5.10. Descriptions of processes, data flows, data stores, and external entities

Descriptions of Primitive Process

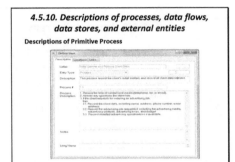

S69

### 4.5.9. Scope of system and lower level DFD

- The number of levels of decomposition depends on the **scope** of the system.
- It is rare to have cases with more than seven levels for a project.

S72

### 4.5.10. Descriptions of processes, data flows, data stores, and external entities (cont'd)

Descriptions of External Entity

S73

### 4.5.10. Descriptions of processes, data flows, data stores, and external entities (cont'd)

**Descriptions of Data Flow**

Copyright Shouhong Wang 2011

---

S76

### 4.5.11. Validating DFD and common errors (cont'd)

(1) Syntax errors in the individual DFDs.

| DFD with Syntax Errors | Explanation | Correct DFD |
|---|---|---|
| A → B | A direct connection between external entities is not a concern of the system | A → P → B |
| A → D | A connection between an external entity and a data store has to go through a process of the system | A → P → D |
| P | A process must have at least one input | → P → |
| → P | A process must have at least one output | → P → |
| X → P → Y | A process must outreact the input into output, and the names of input and output must not be the same | X → P → Y |
| → D | A data store must be used by a process | → D → |
| A → B | A two-headed arrow is not allowed, even though the data flow names are the same | → D → |

Copyright Shouhong Wang 2011

---

S74

### 4.5.10. Descriptions of processes, data flows, data stores, and external entities (cont'd)

**Descriptions of Data Store**

---

S77

### 4.5.11. Validating DFD and common errors (cont'd)

(2) Syntax errors in the decomposition: **Balancing**

(3) Syntax errors in the entire analysis project:

The entire analysis project must use the standard names of the DFD elements across the entire analysis project.

Copyright Shouhong Wang 2011

---

S75

### 4.5.11. Validating DFD and common errors

- **Syntax errors** : violation of "grammatical" rules.

- **semantic errors**: not "grammatical" errors, but are the misrepresentation of the meaning of the system.

Copyright Shouhong Wang 2011

---

S78

### 4.6. The Use of DFD for Systems Acquisition Development

**4.6.1. Contrasting the As-Is and To-Be systems**

As-IS                    To-Be

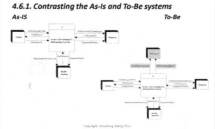

Copyright Shouhong Wang 2011

---

229

S79

### 4.6.1. Contrasting the As-Is and To-Be systems (cont'd)

*As-IS*

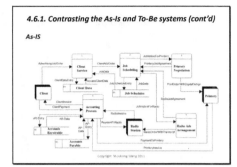

Copyright Shouhong Wang 2011

S80

### 4.6.1. Contrasting the As-Is and To-Be systems (cont'd)

*To-Be*

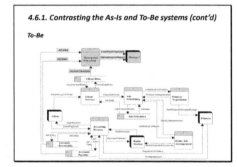

S81

### 4.6.1. Contrasting the As-Is and To-Be systems (cont'd)

- To make the contrast of the as-is system and the to-be system easy to observe, the layouts of the DFDs at the corresponding levels should be alike.
- Technically, the use of copy-paste operations in the CASE tool environment not only saves time, but also, more importantly, makes the two sets of DFDs consistent.

Copyright Shouhong Wang 2011

S82

### 4.6.2. Specifying Functional Requirements for System Design

**(1) Business process:**
- The DFDs themselves

**(2) User-perceived information:**
- The DFDs themselves  .

Copyright Shouhong Wang 2011

S83

### 4.6.2. Specifying Functional Requirements for System Design (cont'd)

(3) **Business rules:**
- A **workflow** is a sequence of operations of a routine which has its start point and end point.
- A **decision** is the selection of a course of action among several alternative actions in response to a certain condition(s).

Copyright Shouhong Wang 2011

S84

### 4.6.2. Specifying Functional Requirements for System Design (cont'd)

(3) **Business rules:**

**Workflow** – A fragment of DFD for an operational sequence.

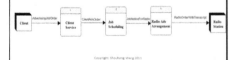

Copyright Shouhong Wang 2011

S85

### 4.6.2. Specifying Functional Requirements for System Design (cont'd)

(3) **Business rules:**

**Decision rules** – In process descriptions.

Decision Rules

Copyright Shouhong Wang 2011

---

S86

### 4.7. Data Modeling

- **Entity-Relationship Diagram (ERD)** for data modeling.
- For system acquisition, data modeling is not really needed.
- This part is fully covered by an independent database course.

Copyright Shouhong Wang 2011

---

S87

### 4.8. Systems Analysis Report

- A **system analysis report** is a documentation of system requirements for the to-be system.
- The complete definition of the project scope.
- The problem analysis of the as-is system, and the objective of the to-be system.
- The system requirements analysis, including all information collected by the requirements process.

Copyright Shouhong Wang 2011

---

S88

### 4.8. Systems Analysis Report (cont'd)

- The business process models of the as-is system and the to-be system. If the system project is systems construction development, the data model for the to-be system should also be included.
- A proposal for the systems design phase.
- The systems analysis report must go through an approval process in accordance with the structure and rules of the organizational.

Copyright Shouhong Wang 2011

---

S89

### Your Project

- 1. Draw the context DFD for the as-is system, and the context DFD for the to-be system.
- 2. Decompose the context diagrams into Level 1 DFD. Keep balancing and eliminate syntax errors. Each group member contributes her/his segments.

Copyright Shouhong Wang 2011

---

S90

### Your Project (cont'd)

- 3. Each group member examines at least one process in the Level 1 DFD and decomposes it into a Level 2 DFD.
- 4. Highlight the differences between the as-is system and the to-be system in the aspects of BPA and BPI.
- 5. Describe the primitive processes.
- 6. Summarize the systems analysis results.

Copyright Shouhong Wang 2011

S1

# CHAPTER 5.
# SYSTEMS DESIGN

Copyright Shouhong Wang 2012

S4

### 5.1. Systems Design for Systems Acquisition Development

- **Systems design for systems acquisition** development is the process of defining the specifications of
- system infrastructure,
- system architecture,
- alternatives software products for the to-be system to satisfy the determined system requirements.

Copyright Shouhong Wang 2011

S2

### CHAPTER 5. SYSTEMS DESIGN

- The **systems design phase** determines how the to-be system is created and how it will operate in terms of hardware, software, networking, system personnel, and operational procedures.
- The objective of the systems design phase is to create a set of system specifications for the to-be system.
- A **system specification** is a structured collection of information that describes all technological components needed for the to-be system to accomplish the system requirements modeled in the systems analysis report.

Copyright Shouhong Wang 2012

S5

### 5.1.1. System infrastructure design

- **System infrastructure** refers to the basic physical structures and organizational information technology (IT) competence needed for the operation of an information system.

Copyright Shouhong Wang 2011

S3

**The systems design phase has three interactive design tasks.**

(1) Designing the system infrastructure for the to-be system.

(2) Designing the alternatives of commercialized software products for the to-be system in systems acquisition development; or, designing the application software specifications for the to-be system in systems construction development.

(3) Designing the system architecture, and selecting hardware and networking of the to-be system.

Copyright Shouhong Wang 2011

S6

### 5.1.1. System infrastructure design (cont'd)

**Basic physical structures** of system infrastructure include

- technical facilities of the information system;
- computing tools;
- equipment storage;
- power;
- telecommunication; and others.

Copyright Shouhong Wang 2011

**S7**

### 5.1.1. System infrastructure design (cont'd)

**Organizational IT competence** includes
- Current and potential users' computer literacy;
- Current and potential users' information literacy;
- procedures, policy, and rules relevant to information systems;
- computing support facilities; and others.

**S10**

### 5.1.2. Design of alternatives of application software products (cont'd)

(1) **Exploring** the software market.

(2) **Confining** the candidate products to generate a short list of alternatives (e.g., three alternatives).

(3) **Examining** the alternatives in great detail against the system requirements.

(4) **Making a recommendation** for the selection of application software product for the to-be system.

**S8**

### 5.1.1. System infrastructure design (cont'd)

- A **system infrastructure design** determines the specifications of the system infrastructure for the to-be system.
- It is rather artistic, and needs great managerial skills to address these attributes of system infrastructure for the organization.

**S11**

### Exploring

- For a large information system, ERP systems are ideal.
- There are a few popular large ERP systems such as
- SAP
- Oracle Applications
- The Sage Group.
- There are also small scale ERP systems: Microsoft Dynamics.
- Open-source ERP systems are widely available , such as
- Compiere
- PostBooks
- Opentaps
- webERP
- OpenERP
- OpenBravo

**S9**

### 5.1.2. Design of alternatives of application software products

- In its broad sense, **design** refers to making a plan.
- Making a plan to choose an ideal application software product on the software market for the to-be system is the system design of systems acquisition development.

**S12**

### Exploring (cont'd)

- For middle and small scale systems, packaged off-the-shelf application software products are ideal.
- Search engines (such as <*www.Google.com*> and <*www.Bing.com*>) are useful.
- Using the keywords relating to information systems of the business concerned (such as *"advertising agent management information system software"*).
- Examine the demo of the software package.
- The system analysts may also consult with IT consultants and software vendors to explore packaged software products.

S13

**Roles of System Analysts in Application Software Selection**

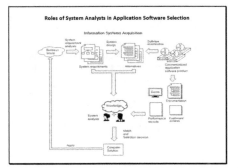

S16

**Decision Matrix for Nonfunctional Requirements**

| Non-Functional Requirement | Weight | Alternative1 | Alternative 2 | Alternative 3 |
|---|---|---|---|---|
| 1. Usability | | | | |
| 1.1. Easy to use - Quality of the user interface design | | | | |
| 1.2. Error tolerance | | | | |
| 1.3. Documentation (reference document, manuals, and tutorial) | | | | |
| 2. Security | | | | |
| 3. Vendor | | | | |
| 3.1. Reputation | | | | |
| 3.2. Services | | | | |
| 3.3. Business alliance | | | | |
| 3.4. Training availability | | | | |
| 3.5. Standardization | | | | |
| 4. Performance | | | | |
| 2.1. Reliability | | | | |
| 2.2. Scalability | | | | |
| 2.3. Speed | | | | |
| 5. Others | | | | |
| 5.1. Multiple language | | | | |
| 5.2. Pricing competitiveness | | | | |
| **Total Scores** | | | | |

Copyright Shouhong Wang 2011

S14

### 5.1.2. Design of alternatives of application software products (cont'd)

- A **decision matrix** is a table of decision factors and their values that allows the system design team to systematically identify, analyze, and rate the relationships between the factors.
- Decision matrix is used to describe a **multiple criteria decision making** problem.

Copyright Shouhong Wang 2011

S17

### 5.1.2. Design of alternatives of application software products (cont'd)

- **Weighted average method** assigns a relative importance weight to each decision criterion.

Copyright Shouhong Wang 2011

S15

**Decision Matrix for Functional Requirements**

| Functionality | Weight | Alternative1 | Alternative 2 | Alternative 3 |
|---|---|---|---|---|
| P1. Client Service | | | | |
| P1.1. Initial Contact and Record Client Data | | | | |
| P1.2. File Advertising Job Order | | | | |
| P1.3. Client Inquiry Process | | | | |
| P1.4. Inform Client Job Schedule | | | | |
| P1.5. Change Advertising Job Order | | | | |
| P2. Job Scheduling | | | | |
| P2.1. | | | | |
| P2.2. | | | | |
| ....... | | | | |
| P3. Accounting Process | | | | |
| P3.1. | | | | |
| P3.2. | | | | |
| P4. Printery Negotiation | | | | |
| P4.1. | | | | |
| P4.2. | | | | |
| P5. Radio Ads Arrangement | | | | |
| P5.1. | | | | |
| P5.2. | | | | |
| ....... | | | | |
| P6. | | | | |
| P6.1. | | | | |
| P6.2. | | | | |
| **Total Scores** | 1 | | | |

Copyright Shouhong Wang 2011

S18

### 5.1.3. Comprehensive decision making for system acquisition

- Since the selection of commercial software product is crucial for the to-be system, in many cases, the project team's design of alternative software products and its recommendation may not be the final decision for the system development, and a comprehensive decision making process in the entire organization is needed.

Copyright Shouhong Wang 2011

S19

### 5.1.3. Comprehensive decision making for system acquisition (cont'd)

- Software product selection is a typical **multiple criteria decision making** problem.
- There have been many models of multiple criteria decision making models. Each model has its advantages and limitations.
- More importantly, the concept of multiple criteria decision making is evolving into a broader notion of decision process serving as knowledge sharing and collaboration in the organization.

Copyright: Shouhong Wang 2011

S20

### 5.1.3. Comprehensive decision making for system acquisition (cont'd)

- **Analytical Hierarchy Process (AHP)** is the most feasible, established, and widely applied method in this case.
- It is actually an extension of the simple weighted average decision matrix method.

Copyright: Shouhong Wang 2011

S21

### 5.1.3. Comprehensive decision making for system acquisition (cont'd) – General criteria hierarchy

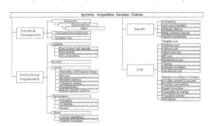

S22

### 5.1.3. Comprehensive decision making for system acquisition (cont'd) – AHP steps

- Step 1: Construct a hierarchy of system aspects for the system acquisition.
- Step 2: Starting from the top of the hierarch, for each sub-tree of the hierarchy, conduct the pairwise comparison by the decision team to reveal the comparative importance between the two aspects.
- Step 3: Using the principal eigenvector of the pairwise comparison matrix manipulated by scaling ratio, find the comparative weight among the aspects for the sub-tree.
- Step 4: Repeat the comparisons from top of the hierarchy until all relative weights have been determined.
- Step 5: For each of the system alternatives, assign the values to each of the hierarchical system aspects. The values could be objective data, or subjective estimations.
- Step 6: Based on the relative weights of the system aspects and the values of the system aspects for each systems alternative, calculate the score of each system alternative. The system with the highest score will be the best decision for system acquisition.

Copyright: Shouhong Wang 2011

S23

### 5.1.4. Backward-design

- The selected commercial application software product may not have an exact match of its functionalities to the system requirements.
- System **backward-design** is the process to fully investigate the difference between what are needed as specified in the system requirements and what are available in the selected application software product and to design an approach to coping with the difference for the system implementation.

Copyright: Shouhong Wang 2011

S24

### 5.1.4. Backward-design (cont'd)

- The system backward-design can explore new BPI components for the to-be system, including
- new operational processes;
- new supporting processes;
- new managerial processes; and
- new information resources.

Copyright: Shouhong Wang 2011

S25

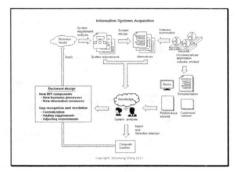

S26

### 5.1.4. Backward-design (cont'd)
## Gap recognition and resolution

- A **gap** refers to the shortfall disparity between the functionalities and features of the recommended commercial software product and the system requirements determined by the system analysis.
- **Gap recognition and resolution** is the process that the system design team identifies the gap and makes plan to close the gap.

Copyright Shouhong Wang 2011

S27

**Gap recognition and resolution (cont'd)**

**(1) Customizing the software product**
- **Customizing** actually transforms the product software in tailor-made software, because the software product in its standardized form causes a gap for the to-be system.
- In most cases of small and middle size business, customizing is not an option.

Copyright Shouhong Wang 2011

S28

**Gap recognition and resolution (cont'd)**

**(2) Adding supplemental software product**
- Adding a supplemental software product will certainly increase the cost.
- More importantly, the data compatibility and the interfaces between the central application software and the supplemental software could be complicated.

Copyright Shouhong Wang 2011

S29

**Gap recognition and resolution (cont'd)**

**(3) Adjusting system requirements**
- **Adjusting system requirements** is more sensible for causing potential resistance in the usage of the recommended software product.

Copyright Shouhong Wang 2011

S30

### 5.1.5. System architecture design
- **System architecture** refers to the structure of a computational resources network.
- Topology of computational recourses:
- Hardware (PCs, servers, routers, switches, and printers and other peripheral equipment).
- Operating systems.
- Database
- Application programs across the computer network.

Copyright Shouhong Wang 2011

S31

### Network diagram (no standard)

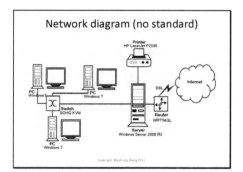

S32

### Computing Equipment Layout Plan

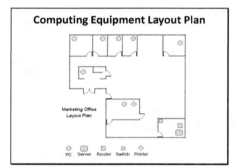

S33

### Specifications of computer

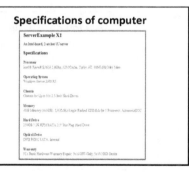

S34

#### 5.1.5. System architecture design (cont'd)

- In an *ideal* cloud computing environment, it is no longer for ordinary business organizations to own and manage their systems architecture.
- Cloud computing provides computational power, software, data access, and storages as services through the Internet.
- Although the perceived advantages of the cloud computing model are extraordinary, cloud computing technology is still in its very early stage.

S35

#### 5.2. Systems Design for Systems Construction Development

- **Systems design for systems construction development is the process of defining the specifications for the system infrastructure, the system architecture and its components, the database, the user interface, and the program modules for constructing the to-be system to satisfy the determined system requirements.**

S36

#### 5.2. Systems Design for Systems Construction Development (cont'd)

- System infrastructure design for systems construction is not much different from system infrastructure design for systems acquisition development.
- When designing the system architecture for systems construction development, the system development team can have more flexibility in choosing hardware and networking because compatibility constraints can be relaxed through the application software construction.

S37

### 5.2.1. Design of physical business process model

- A **logical business process model** illustrates the essential requirements for the system but does not specify how these essential requirements can be accomplished.
- A **physical business process model** specifies systems construction details and to document how the logical business process model can be implemented using software construction techniques.

Copyright Shouhong Wang 2011

S40

### 5.2.2. Database design

- **Database design** is to determine how data is stored and accessed.
- Database design includes database logical design and database physical design.
- Detailed database design techniques are normally taught in an independent database course and the companion textbooks.

Copyright Shouhong Wang 2011

S38

**5.2.1. Design of physical business process model (cont'd)**

- A physical business processing model contains the same components as the logical business process model, and also includes additional technical details for construction such as
- computerized process and data stores;
- user-system boundary;
- computer programming languages used for construction;
- data communication and data transmission media; and
- database management systems.

Copyright Shouhong Wang 2011

S41

### 5.2.3. User interface design

- The user interface of the system allows the users to access the system through
- **input** - to enter data for operating the system;
- **output** - to receive information from the system; and
- **navigation** - to find a direction of action.

Copyright Shouhong Wang 2011

S39

**5.2.1. Design of physical business process model (cont'd)**

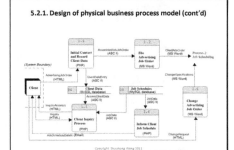

Copyright Shouhong Wang 2011

S42

### 5.2.3. User interface design (cont'd)

(1) The **user interface structure design** –
User interface structure diagram

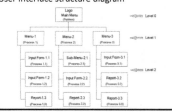

S43

### 5.2.3. User interface design (cont'd)

(2) The **user interface view design** defines the **GUI** (Graphical User Interface) screens and the report layouts.

- Simplicity
- Visibility
- Informing
- Tolerance
- Consistency
- Inviting

Copyright: Shouhong Wang 2011

S44

### 5.2.4. Programs design

- Structured programming design (e.g., for C and COBOL languages)
- Object-oriented programming design (e.g., for VB.NET and Java languages)
- This part is taught in Programming courses

Copyright: Shouhong Wang 2011

S45

### 5.3. Systems Design Report

- The system infrastructure design.
- The system architecture specifications, including hardware, networking, and operating systems.
- The application software specifications.
  For systems acquisition:
  - The alternatives of software products;
  - Demos and trial records ;
  - Supporting documents ;
  - The decision matrices;
  - The gap resolution ;
  - The comprehensive decision.

Copyright: Shouhong Wang 2011

S46

### 5.3. Systems Design Report (cont'd)

For systems construction:
- The physical business process models for the to-be system;
- The database design for the to-be system;
- The user interface design for the to-be system;
- The programs design for the to-be system; and
- The recommended computational instruments (i.e., the database management systems, computer programming languages, and other software tools.) for the construction.

Copyright: Shouhong Wang 2011

S47

### 5.3. Systems Design Report (cont'd)

- Proposal for the systems implementation phase.
- The systems design report must go through an approval process in accordance with the structure and rules of the organization.

Copyright: Shouhong Wang 2011

S48

### Your Project

- 1. Search application software products alternatives for the to-be system.
- 2. Select three most impressive application software products alternatives.
- 3. Examine the three alternatives and develop decision matrices of functional requirements and nonfunctional requirements.
- 4. Select one of the alternatives.

Copyright: Shouhong Wang 2011

S49

**Your Project (cont'd)**

- 5. Search hardware which compatible with the selected software product for the to-be system.
- 6. Search networking equipment for the to-be system.
- 7. Summarize the system design results.

Copyright Zhoushang Wang 2011

S1

# CHAPTER 6.
# SYSTEMS IMPLEMENTATION

Copyright Shouhong Wang 2011

S4

## 6.1. System Implementation for Systems Acquisition Development

**6.1.1. System installation**

**6.1.2. Configuring ERP system, or customizing software product**

**6.1.3. Data conversion**

- Identify the data for conversion.
- Determine data conversion timing.
- Decide the new data formats.
- Select data conversion methods and tools.
- Define data archiving policies and procedures.

Copyright Shouhong Wang 2011

S2

## CHAPTER 6. SYSTEMS IMPLEMENTATION

- The **systems implementation phase** builds the to-be system based on the system specifications provided by the design phase, and converts the as-is system to the to-be system.

Copyright Shouhong Wang 2011

S5

## 6.1. System Implementation for Systems Acquisition Development (cont'd)

**6.1.4. System tests for acquired system**

- Functional requirement tests
- Reliability tests
- Usability tests
- Performance tests
- Error handling tests
- Security tests
- Scalability tests

Copyright Shouhong Wang 2011

S3

## Systems Implementation

(1) Generating the to-be system.
- For systems acquisition development, installation of the software product, configuring or making customization if needed, and data conversion are the major tasks of this step.
- For systems construction development, the actual construction for the to-be system through the use of computer tools takes place.

(2) Converting the as-is system to the to-be system, and testing the to-be system.

(3) Establishing system support facilities for the new information system.

(4) Documenting the systems implementation.

Copyright Shouhong Wang 2011

S6

## 6.2. System Construction for Systems Construction Development

- 6.2.1. Database construction and tests (extensive!).
- 6.2.2. Application software programming and tests (extensive and time consuming!).
- 6.2.3. Hardware and network installation.
- 6.2.4. Data conversion.
- 6.2.5. System tests for constructed system.
  - User acceptance tests (UAT)
    - Alpha testing
    - Beta testing

Copyright Shouhong Wang 2011

S7

### 6.3. Transition from As-Is System to To-Be System

- Select system conversion method.
- Determine a contingency plan in case the conversion fails.
- Schedule user training.
- Establish system support facilities.
- Hand-over to the system operation team.

Copyright Shouhong Wang 2011

S10

### Contingency Plan

- What problems could occur during the conversion;
- The conditions, the likelihood, and the consequences of these problems; and
- How the organization can prevent major business disruptions if problems occur during the conversion.

Copyright Shouhong Wang 2011

S8

### 6.3.1. New policies and procedures for the new system

- Descriptions of the new policies and procedures.
- Rationale of the new policies and procedures.
- "Roadmap" for directions and steps that users can follow to carry out the new procedures.
- Users responsibilities and consequences of violation of the new policies and procedures.
- Pointers to help assistance.

Copyright Shouhong Wang 2011

S11

### 6.3.3. User training

- **Technical users** are people who are responsible for the maintenance and operation of the system after the new system starts.
- **End-users** are non-technical people who use the system but are not responsible for the problems of the system.

Copyright Shouhong Wang 2011

S9

### 6.3.2. System conversion methods and contingency plans

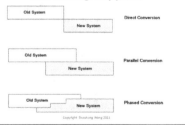

Copyright Shouhong Wang 2011

S12

### 6.4. Establishing System Support Facilities and System Hand-Over

**Common system support facilities:**
- online frequently asked questions (FAQs);
- online documents (operation manuals, references, and tutorials);
- online help;
- telephone help desk;
- problem reporting channel, and specific support team members for handling problems and maintenance work orders.

**Hands-over to the system operations-maintenance team**

Copyright Shouhong Wang 2011

S13

### 6.5. Systems Implementation Report

- System installation records;
- System acceptance tests records;
- System conversion records;
- Reference manuals;
- Operation manuals;
- User training records; and
- Official hand-over document.

S14

### Your Project

- 1. Discuss the implementation process for the new system of your course project.
- 2. Specify the method of data conversion that could be used for the new system of your course project.
- 3. Discuss user training for your course project.
- 4. Select a system conversion method for your course project.
- 5. Discuss your plan of system tests for your course project.
- 6. Discuss the support facilities after the new system starts to operate for your course project.

S1

# CHAPTER 7.
# SYSTEMS MAINTENANCE

Copyright Shouhong Wang 2011

S2

## CHAPTER 7. SYSTEMS MAINTENANCE

- The **systems maintenance phase** improves the new information system. It includes the following major activities.
- (1) System support and system maintenance management.
- (2) Post-project evaluation.
- (3) Preparation for the next new information system.

Copyright Shouhong Wang 2011

S3

## 7.1. Management of User Support and System Maintenance

***7.1.1. User support*** – training and helping
***7.1.2. System maintenance procedure***
**System maintenance** refers to an activity that makes changes to the system in response to new business needs or reported deficiency of the system.
- Corrective maintenance.
- Adaptive maintenance.
- Perfective maintenance.
- Preventive maintenance.

Copyright Shouhong Wang 2011

S4

## System maintenance procedure

(1) The user or the help desk experiences a problem and files a request for changes, and sends the request to the system support and maintenance team manager.
(2) The maintenance team analyzes the request and checks its validity. It develops a maintenance solution to the problem or rejects the request for changes.
(3) The maintenance job takes in place.
(4) The maintenance team works with the users to test the result of maintenance to ensure the problem has been solved.

Copyright Shouhong Wang 2011

S5

(cont'd)

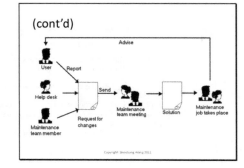

Copyright Shouhong Wang 2011

S6

## 7.2. Post-Project Evaluation

- Post-project evaluation examines whether the system development project has achieved its objectives.

Copyright Shouhong Wang 2011

S7

## 7.2. Post-Project Evaluation (cont'd)

The **metrics** for post-project evaluation include:

- the planned system scope and the actual system scope;
- the expected functional requirements and the actual system functionalities;
- the expected nonfunctional requirements and the actual system features;
- the users' satisfaction;
- the overall system usability;
- the overall system efficiency performance; and
- the expected financial performance and the actual financial performance.

S9

Once the system maintenance costs reach to high, and the performance of the system becomes relative inferior given the advances of new information technology, a new information system project is to be initiated and the SDLC starts a new cycle.

S8

## 7.3. Preparation of Planning for the Next New System

**System maintenance team retains important information of the current system:**

- Long standing problems of the system.
- Maintenance costs of the system.
- Performance of the system in comparison with similar systems.
- The potential **legacy system** for the next generation system.

S10

## Your Project

- 1. Discuss the user support issues for the new system of your course project.
- 2. Discuss the system maintenance issues for the new system of your course project.
- 3. Discuss how you would conduct a post-project evaluation for your course project.
- 4. Discuss how you would collect information for the long-term consideration of system development in the organization after the new system of your course project starts to operate.

S1

**APPENDIX A.**

**GUIDELINE FOR**

**SYSTEMS ACQUISITION**

**PROJECTS**

S3

**2. Learning Objective of the Project**

The learning objective of the project is to analyze and design a computerized information system for a small/middle size business organization. The company must be real and approachable. Small business with little support of computerized information system is ideal for this project.

S2

**1. Project Scheme**

S4

**Deliverables**

- **Project Proposal**
- **Project Presentations**
- **Project Report**

S1

## APPENDIX B.
## CASE TOOL:
## VISIBLE ANALYST

S4

### 2. Visible Analyst

- Visible Analyst, a product of Visible Systems Corporation, is a CASE tool.
- It has been widely used in many industrial organizations as well as educational institutions.

S2

### 1. CASE Tools

- **CASE (Computer Aided Systems Engineering** or **Computer Aided Software Engineering)** tools are a category of software that supports the information systems development process.
- The central component of a CASE tool is the **CASE repository** that stores all diagrams and project information, and is shared by all project team members.

S5

### A. Login

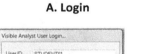

S3

### 1. CASE Tools (cont'd)

- A CASE tool can be used to coordinate project team activities, and to facilitate knowledge sharing among the project team members.
- A CASE tool allows the project team to follow the standard terminology.
- A CASE tool is not just a computer drawing tool. It can have intelligent features to verify the systems analysis and design results to a certain degree.
- A CASE tool can generate consistent documents with detailed information for each phase of the SDLC. Thus, a CASE tool can make the systems development process more efficient.

S6

### B. File menu

S7

### C. Create a new project

S8

### D. Create a DFD

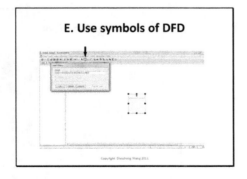

S9

### E. Use symbols of DFD

S10

### Process

S11

### External entity

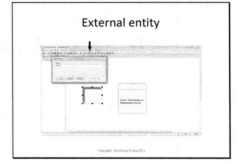

S12

### Data flow

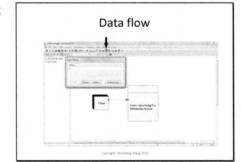

S13

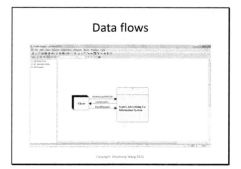

Data flows

S16

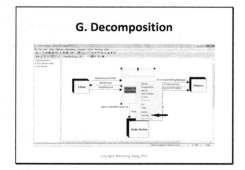

**G. Decomposition**

S14

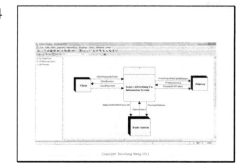

S17

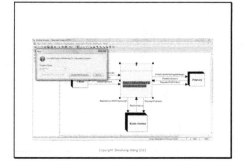

S15

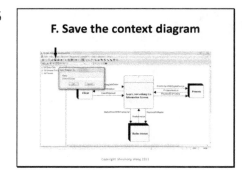

**F. Save the context diagram**

S18

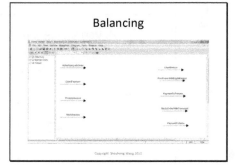

Balancing

S19

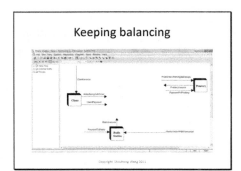

S20

S21

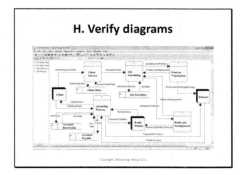

S22

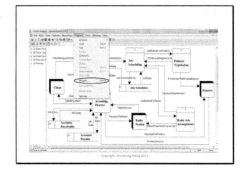

S23

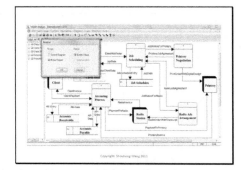

S24

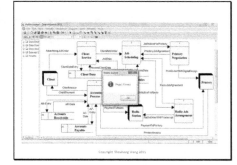

S25

**I. Define entities, data flows, data stores, and processes**

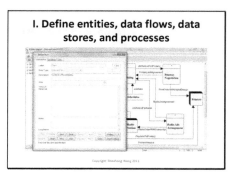

S28

**J. Repository**

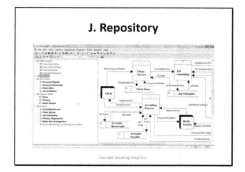

S26

S29

**K. Color**

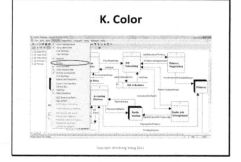

S27

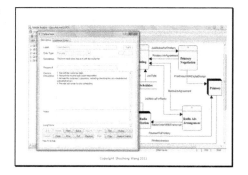

S30

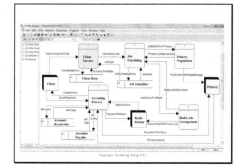

S31

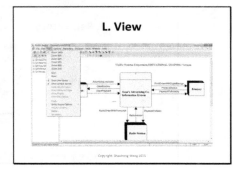

S33

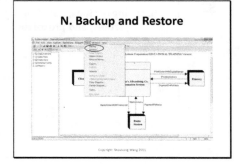

S32

### M. Copy-pasting diagrams

- Open the context DFD diagram of AS-IS.
- Choose Edit on the top menu, and then choose Select All on the pull-down menu to enclose all diagram lines and symbols within a bounding box.
- Choose Edit on the top menu, and then Copy to copy the diagram to the Windows clipboard. Nothing happens on the screen.
- Create a new project (TO-BE) using the same DFD Rule set.
- Create a new Context DFD in the TO-BE project, and type a name for the process, say, TOBE. This process name is automatically added to a context level diagram.
- Save the diagram with a name, say, TOBE-Context.
- Right mouse click on the process TOBE, and choose Delete on the pop-up menu.
- Save the diagram again.
- Choose Edit on the top menu, and then choose Paste on the pull-down menu. The AS-IS context diagram is pasted onto the TOBE-Context diagram.
- Save the diagram again.
- Right mouse click on the TOBE process, and the Explode option is enabled which allows you to decompose the context diagram.
- Repeat the above procedure for the Level-1 DFD and Level-2 DFDs.
- After two identical sets of DFDs are created, it is possible to add, delete, or color any symbols in the DFDs of the TO-BE project.

S1

# APPENDIX C.
# AN EXAMPLE OF SYSTEMS
# ANALYSIS AND DESIGN

(Note: This case example describes key
components of systems analysis and design
for systems acquisition development. It is
not a complete project report. A detailed
guideline of course project is exhibited in
Appendix A.)

Copyright Shouhong Wang 2011

S4

Figure C-3. Level-1 Diagram of the As-Is System

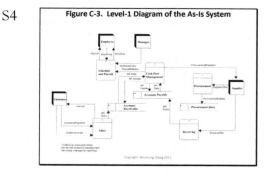

S2

Figure C-1. Context Diagram of the As-Is System

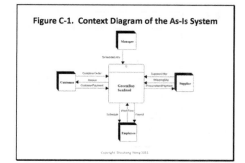

S5

Figure C-4. Level-1 Diagram of the To-Be System

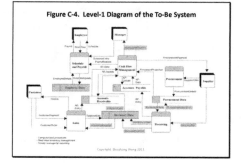

S3

Figure C-2. Context Diagram of the To-Be System

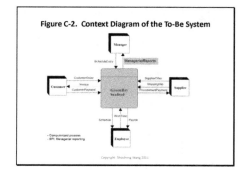

S6

Figure C-5. Level-2 Diagram of Process-1 (Sales) of the To-Be System

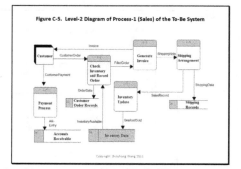

S7

### Figure C-6. Primitive Process Descriptions for Processes 1.1 - 1.5

| Process | Descriptions |
|---------|--------------|
| P1.1. Check Inventory and Record Order | Check the inventory against the customer's order. If the inventory is sufficient Then record the customer's order Else record the back order and send a notice to the customer. |
| P1.2. Generate Invoice | Estimate the price of the seafood order. Estimate the shipping cost. Generate an invoice for the customer. |
| P1.3. Shipping Arrangement | Generate a shipping order. Record the shipping data. Update the inventory. |
| P1.4. Payment Process | Check the payment against the invoice. Update accounts receivable. Banking the check. |
| P1.5. Inventory Update | Deduct the amount of seafood from the inventory file. |

Copyright Shouhong Wang 2011

S10

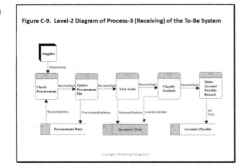

Figure C-9. Level-2 Diagram of Process-3 (Receiving) of the To-Be System

Copyright Shouhong Wang 2011

S8

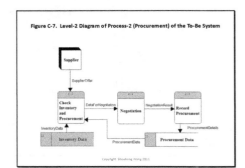

Figure C-7. Level-2 Diagram of Process-2 (Procurement) of the To-Be System

Copyright Shouhong Wang 2011

S11

### Figure C-10. Primitive Process Descriptions for Processes 3.1 - 3.5

| Process | Descriptions |
|---------|--------------|
| P3.1. Check Procurement | Retrieve the procurement record against the shipping slip. Check the procurement record. Find any disparity between the shipping slip and the procurement record. |
| P3.2. Update Procurement File | Include the shipping slip data into the procurement file. Record the disparity. |
| P3.3. Tare Scale | Weight the shipped seafood. Deduct tank's weight. Weight data are recorded to the inventory database in real-time. |
| P3.4. Classify Seafood | Measure the seafood product. Record the class data to the inventory database. |
| P3.5. Make Accounts Payable Record | Calculate the cost of the received seafood product. Create an accounts payable record for the supplier. |

Copyright Shouhong Wang 2011

S9

### Figure C-8. Primitive Process Descriptions for Processes 2.1 - 2.3

| Process | Descriptions |
|---------|--------------|
| P2.1. Check Inventory and Procurement | Check the inventory against the supplier's offer. If the inventory is low Start negotiation Else decline the offer. |
| P2.2. Negotiation | Negotiate the seafood price. If the price is appropriate Send a procurement agreement Else decline the offer. |
| P2.3. Record Procurement | Acquire details of the supplier's offer. Record the data to the procurement file. |

Copyright Shouhong Wang 2011

S12

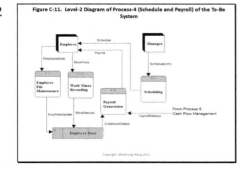

Figure C-11. Level-2 Diagram of Process-4 (Schedule and Payroll) of the To-Be System

Copyright Shouhong Wang 2011

254

S13

### Figure C-12. Primitive Process Descriptions for Processes 4.1 - 4.4

| Process | Descriptions |
|---|---|
| P4.1. Employee File Maintenance | Record the employee profile. Update the employee profile if there is a change. |
| P4.2. Work Times Recording | Record the work hours daily for each employee. |
| P4.3. Payroll Generation | Upon the release of payroll and bonus, Calculate payroll for each employee. Write checks for each employee. |
| P4.4. Scheduling | Manager enters scheduling data. Advise the schedule to each employee. |

Copyright Shouhong Wang 2011

S16

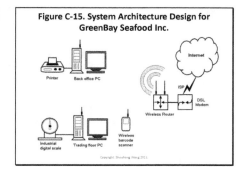

### Figure C-15. System Architecture Design for GreenBay Seafood Inc.

Copyright Shouhong Wang 2011

S14

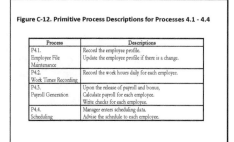

### Figure C-13. Level-2 Diagram of Process-5 (Cash Follow Management) of the To-Be System

Copyright Shouhong Wang 2011

S17

### Figure C-16. Exercise Decision Matrix of Functional Requirements for the GreenBay Seafood Example

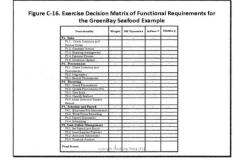

Copyright Shouhong Wang 2011

S15

### Figure C-14. Primitive Process Descriptions for Processes 5.1 - 5.4

| Process | Descriptions |
|---|---|
| P5.1. Set Payroll and Bonus | Check accounts payable and accounts receivable. Set a limit for payroll and bonus. |
| P5.2. Issue Supplier Payment | Check accounts payable and accounts receivable. Write a check for a due payment for supplier. |
| P5.3. Accounts Adjustment | Record expenses or income other than sales or procurement. |
| P5.4. Financial Analysis | Check accounts payable and accounts receivable. Generate daily and weekly cash flow projection. Check the inventory and procurement data. Generate financial statements. Generate customer sales and payment analysis reports. Generate inventory analysis reports. Generate procurement analysis reports. |

Copyright Shouhong Wang 2011

S18

### Figure C-17. Exercise Decision Matrix of Nonfunctional Requirements for the GreenBay Seafood Example

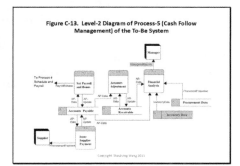

Copyright Shouhong Wang 2011

255

S1

**APPENDIX D.
AN EXAMPLE OPEN SOURCE ERP
SYSTEM** *

<u>*</u> **Acknowledgement:** The screenshots of webERP are reprinted from <www.weberp.org> with permission of Mr. Phil Daintree, the founder of webERP and one of the main contributors.

S4

Open Source ERP Systems (cont'd)

- A business model behind an open source ERP system is a win-win relationship between the business community, the partner network, and the software editors.

S2

### 1. Overview of ERP Systems

- A large scale ERP system such as SAP, Oracle Applications, and The Sage Group is used for large business organizations.
- Microsoft Dynamics is suitable for medium-sized business organizations with up to about 2,250 users.
- Recently, open source ERP systems are widely available for medium or even small business organizations, such as webERP, Compiere, PostBooks, Opentaps, OpenERP, and OpenBravo.

S5

webERP (www.weberp.org)

- webERP is a complete Web-based ERP system with emphasis on accounting.
- The open source ERP system requires only a Web-browser and PDF reader to use.
- webERP is a pioneer of "**cloud computing**".

S3

Open Source ERP Systems

- An open source software product is free to use, and has a copyright license which allows end users to review and modify the source code for their own customization and/or troubleshooting needs.
- Open source licenses are also commonly free. One popular set of free open source software licenses are those approved by the Open Source Initiative (OSI) based on their Open Source Definition (OSD).

S6

webERP (www.weberp.org) (cont'd)

- Order entry
- Taxes
- Accounts payable
- Accounts receivable
- Inventory
- Purchasing
- Banking
- General ledger
- Manufacturing
- Contract costing
- Fixed assets

S7

### webERP ([www.weberp.org](www.weberp.org)) (cont'd)

- 1. Community Support - The webERP mailing lists can be accessed via the nabble forum ([www.nabble.com](www.nabble.com)). The users archives and developer archives of the mailing lists contain valuable knowledge.
- 2. Commercial Support - Several companies offer commercial support which may be preferable for ordinary business organizations.

S10

### Payables

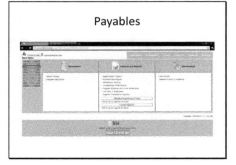

S8

### 3. Sample of user interface of webERP: Sales

S11

### Purchases

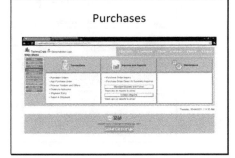

S9

### Receivables

S12

### Inventory

S13

Manufacturing

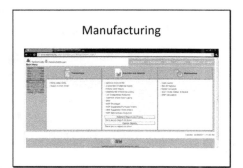

S16

Set up - Configuring

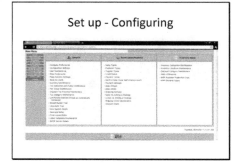

S14

General Ledger

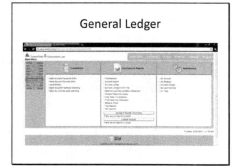

S17

Configuring

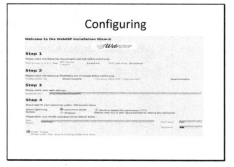

S15

Assets Management

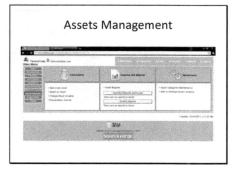

S18

Configuring

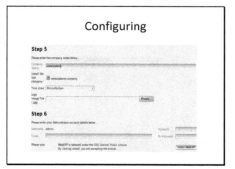

S19

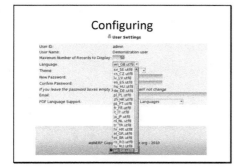

CPSIA information can be obtained
at www.ICGtesting.com
Printed in the USA
BVHW08s0333070718
521026BV00003B/17/P